T0276247

TALES FROM A TEACHING LIFE

Cover image: "Magic book on grunge background" by D-Keine, courtesy of Getty Images

Printed in the United States of America on acid-free paper
First edition

UNIVERSITY OF NEW ORLEANS PRESS
2000 Lakeshore Drive
New Orleans, Louisiana 70148
unopress.org

Library of Congress Cataloging-in-Publication Data

Names: Austin, Patricia, 1950- author.
Title: Tales from a teaching life : vignettes in verse / Patricia Austin.
Description: First edition. | New Orleans : University of New Orleans
    Press, 2023.
Identifiers: LCCN 2023030633 (print) | LCCN 2023030634 (ebook) | ISBN
    9781608012602 (paperback ; acid-free paper) | ISBN 9781608012626 (ebook)

Subjects: LCSH: Teachers--Poetry. | Teaching--Poetry. | LCGFT: Poetry.
Classification: LCC PS3601.U8634 T35 2023 (print) | LCC PS3601.U8634
    (ebook) | DDC 811/.6--dc23/eng/20230801
LC record available at https://lccn.loc.gov/2023030633
LC ebook record available at https://lccn.loc.gov/2023030

TALES FROM A TEACHING LIFE

VIGNETTES IN VERSE

PATRICIA AUSTIN

*To Pam, my best friend and the best sister in the universe, for a
lifetime of listening to my stories*

*And in memory of my parents for a lifetime of love
and for instilling in me my love of books
and a sense of loyalty and commitment—
just by who they were and how they lived their lives*

CONTENTS

Prologue

Part I – Where it All Begins, Agnes Scott College Philosophy Major Sans Clues about My Future

Part II – University of New Hampshire Graduate School, Master of Arts in Teaching

Oyster River Elementary

Part III – Elementary Teacher
GEORGIA

Dacula Elementary

Peachtree Elementary

NEW ORLEANS, LOUISIANA

Forest Park Elementary

Hiatus

LOUISIANA – ST. BERNARD PARISH

Arabi Elementary

MISSISSIPPI

West Side Elementary

LOUISIANA – JEFFERSON PARISH

Hazel Park Elementary

Clancy Elementary

Part V Brave New Online World: A Hero's Journey

Part VI Retrospective

Epilogue

Prologue

The Writing

Before the dawn breaks
before the day begins...

Thoughts dart like minnows of the mind
spawning ideas spanning decades

slipping in and out of schools
through hallways, classrooms, closets,

and even cafeterias where I have taught.
Words wander, sometimes landing,

sometimes snagged on a line while
I make meaning of memories—

capturing moments
of a teaching life.

Summer 2019

While most summers as a teacher I worked,
this summer I shed the schedule.
Now, while steamy days spread out
before me like an empty page

    without to-do lists
    without planning or grading
    without deadlines

they also loom
        that empty page

    with too much promise
    with fear that I'll fail
    with too much time in my head.

But I tarry. Let me begin.

Part I

WHERE IT ALL BEGINS
AGNES SCOTT COLLEGE
PHILOSOPHY MAJOR
SANS CLUE ABOUT MY FUTURE

Life's Purpose

One thousand pieces
scattered without a picture
on the box.
Patterns of shape
patterns of color
provided hints
but also
produced frustration
triggered anxiety.

And yet
when images emerged
when one group of pieces
connected to another,
the puzzle
seemed possible.

Volunteering #1

Four of us, as freshmen (faceless now
      I cannot recall all these years later)
volunteered at the school for mentally retarded kids,
      (Yes, cringe, that was the term used at the time)
each of us assigned to help in a different class.

When we slid into the car to head back to campus
the other girls bubbled with enthusiasm.
      "The kids are so adorable."
          "It's so rewarding."
              "I can't wait till next week."

What was wrong with me?

Was I missing some compassion gene?
I felt awkward,
      annoyed when a kid
yanked and broke my necklace.
I wanted to quit.

How did teachers have patience
to repeat the same directions
day after day to see
      no progress
week after week to see
      only glimmers of learning
month after month?

After a while, though,
I felt a little less awkward
             less annoyed.
(I remembered never to wear jewelry.)
After all, I tried convincing myself, I was
another pair of hands, another pair of ears
             one afternoon a week.

So I didn't quit.
(Though all the others did).

Now I bussed to the school
             never loved it but I had
             signed up, made a commitment.

The teacher's face lightened when I arrived.
"It's so nice to have another adult in the room."
             (Was I an adult?)

And seven-year-old Scottie's eyes
lit up when he saw me.
After nine months,
             he could write from one to ten
             he could almost write his name.
Our very last day, heading to the gym,
Scottie slipped his moist hand in mine.
(Damn, I'd forgotten to take off my jewelry.)

Scottie fingered my garnet and looked up at me.
"You have ring," he said, his voice sad.
I looked at him, puzzled. He continued:
"That means I can't marry you when I'm big."

His eyes glistened with tears.
And so did mine.

Volunteering #2

It all started with a sign in the mailroom:
Adult Literacy Program
Make a difference in someone's life—
teach someone to read.
Two-day training required.
All materials provided.

Why not?

We learned first about a world-wide project
developed by Frank Laubach to enhance
literacy in third-world countries,
now, in America. Each one
teach one was the mantra.

Our training began:
Every letter has a name. The name of the letter is "b." Say b.
Every letter has a sound, as well as a name.
The sound of the letter is "bu." Say "bu."
(The trick was to keep the hinted vowel sound
to a whisper, a mere puff of air following the consonant.)
A "b" has a long tail and a circle that looks like a ball. Read "ball."
(The dictum was: You had to say "read ball" not "say ball,"
subtly convincing the students that yes,
they were indeed reading.)
A sentence followed:
This is a ball. Read "This is a ball."

Each consonant. Each vowel.
Each digraph (those pesky ch, sh, and kn kinds of sounds)

had its own patter.
We could not stray from the script.
We chanted as a class.
We practiced with a partner.

I don't know if it's more amazing
that I still remember the script
or how little else I recall.
Was this training just for us college students?
Was it a community project?
Training complete, I was paired
with Mildred, who cleaned the college library,
surrounded, for years, by books
yet unable to read them.

As I launched the lesson, quoting the script,
I remember being embarrassed
by the juvenile pictures, juvenile
patter. Perhaps I even apologized.
She waved that aside, caught on quickly,
and taught me to be more comfortable.

I don't recall how often we met.
I do recall that when we finished
the scripted lessons, Mildred didn't want to stop.
Reading from newspapers,
she did not believe that men
had walked on the moon.
"But there are photos," I insisted.
"They even brought back moon rocks."
"Nonsense," she replied.
"They picked up those rocks in Arizona."

Nothing would convince her otherwise,
but still, she enjoyed reading news.

For three years, we worked
until she picked whatever she wanted
from shelves she dusted.
Her last selection—Margaret Meade.

When I graduated, she gave me
an autographed volume of Robert Frost's poetry
(sadly, lost years later to hurricane floodwaters).
She'd bought it when Frost visited the college.
"This is too much. Too special. I can't take this," I told her.
"You've taught me a lot; I want you to have it," she said.

In hindsight, I see those were my first three years of teaching.
Yet I never thought of it that way—until now.
And it all began with a sign in the mailroom.

Summer at the Lighthouse

It wasn't what I expected
when I volunteered
at the Lighthouse for the Blind.
No, that's silly to say.
I had no idea what to expect.
But it hadn't been this:
Reading a boring sixth grade textbook
into a recorder so it could be transcribed to Braille.

But I'm getting ahead of myself.
The first day was my audition—
reading to Mabel Brouwer.
Her sightless eyes fluttered,
her head bobbed,
but her hands ...
they worked with unimaginable speed
punching each letter
of each word
of each sentence
so that a blind sixth grader
could start school come fall
with a textbook.

Even in 1969, Braille typewriters
were a thing.
But Mabel scoffed
at new technology
clung to the old
claimed she was much faster
using the slate and stylus.

And she was.
As I read aloud, she was my judge:
Was my voice clear?
Could she understand me?
Each punch of the stylus
punctuated the air as I watched
mesmerized.

I passed the test.
So all summer long
I read.
Mabel would later transcribe.

At summer's end, the Lighthouse
presented me with a slate and stylus.
At home, as I attempted to write,
each laborious punch of each letter
made me marvel more at Mabel's skill.

Fast-forward thirty-six summers.
After Hurricane Katrina,
The Times-Picayune published
names of those whose lives were lost.
I spotted a familiar name
Mabel Brouwer—seventy
She would have been about seventy.
How likely
it may have been
that a woman who was blind,
stubborn, and fiercely independent
might have been left behind.

Summer at the YMCA

Figured I'd work alongside
an artsy, craftsy, enthusiastic
teacher who would teach me crafts
and together we would teach kids.

Wrong.

Found out I was to work alongside
a burned out, bitter, lazy
teacher who passed out coloring sheets
and barked at kids to sit and be quiet.

Not my idea (or the kids' idea) of summer camp.
Oodles of untouched crafts packed closets.
"Mind if we pull out some of these supplies?" I asked.
The teacher responded with a suit-yourself shrug.

From splatters of paint in spin art (a favorite)
to tangles of yarn (and some tears) in weaving
to coils of clay and lopsided pots,
the kids and I learned side by side.

Did I resent the teacher who sat on her ass all summer
collecting a paycheck for not working?
You betcha.
Did I have a good time anyway
listening to clamoring cries,
"Miss Pat, how do I…."
"Miss Pat, come help me!"
"Miss Pat, look at mines."

You betcha.

Sometimes the lessons you learn
are not at all the lessons
you think you'll learn.

When I Grow Up…

When I was eight,
I received a *This is Me* book
for recording all things Me.
On the page: *When I grow up,*
> *I want to be* _____
> *But never a* _____

I didn't hesitate to put "writer"
on the *I want to be* blank.
It's not that I wrote a lot.
I read a lot.
I loved libraries
and dreamed of a book
sitting on a shelf,
my name on the spine.

I didn't hesitate to put "teacher"
> on the *but never* blank.
I'd played school with my sister,
but I didn't love school
> and never
wanted to be a teacher.

When I was twenty-one
and received a diploma
> I had to decide for real:

When I grow up, I want to be—

I drew a blank.
What do philosophy majors do?
        I thought and I thought.
I'd fallen in love
with epistemology exploring questions:
        What is knowledge?
        What does it mean to know something?
        How much can we know?
        Do we have limits?
        How do we learn?

Could it be...
that volunteering added up?
        teaching the mentally challenged kids plus
        teaching crafts at the Y plus
        teaching an adult to read?
Could it be
that the very thing
I said I'd never do
would be the thing
I would do?

An Imagined Future

Frayed edges of loneliness
led me down Decatur streets at dusk
      away from institutional days in dorms
      away from friends who fit in,
coeds who cottoned to college life.

Past the houses where professors lived
where lights inside emitted
      the warm yellow glow of home
      reminding me of the home I missed
      with desperation so deep
it sent me down a spiral.
Me, who once relished Byron's
sentiments of alone but not lonely.
      But not here. Not now
        where I was
alone   and lost.

I wound a web of fantasy
around professors' lives in those houses:
the life of the mind
I had grown to love after
high school's intellectual desert.

Life needed
this warm yellow glow of home.
      I wanted that life—
could envision it
in some far off time.

Part II

UNIVERSITY OF NEW HAMPSHIRE
GRADUATE SCHOOL
MASTER OF ARTS IN TEACHING

Grad School Ballad

Take a trip with me to '73
adult life about to begin
as if the next step was finding the key
to where I would go and had been.

There was Boston or Claremont, I could have picked
but Durham had certain appeal
for this teaching future I couldn't predict.
It all felt a bit surreal.

When day one of class was all about feelings,
and getting in touch with ourselves,
I feared I was over my head in dealing
with issues I'd already shelved.

How did this touchy-feely stuff
get us ready to teach?
If only then I'd thought hard enough
how these skills would help me reach

students—instead, I wanted to quit,
sure that I'd made a mistake.
My journals and letters home admit
the choice I had made was at stake.

Week two improved when we set up our space—
my two fellow teachers and me.
When crafting our plans, I felt ready to face
my future, no longer at sea.

Our intrepid troop, where the kids would reign,
gathered each morning in song.
Indeed, with each chorus and each refrain,
maybe I'd found a place to belong.

OYSTER RIVER ELEMENTARY

Teaching Internship

All too quickly, I realized
A. S. Neill's *Summerhill* and
John Dewey's *Democracy and Education*
were harder in practice than theory.

Learning was about commitment
making a choice and sticking with it.
Some of our fourth, fifth, and sixth graders
flitted from choice to choice
quit when a chore challenged them.

While some kids plunged
into intellectual play and reveled in research,
I remember most the ones
who only toyed with topics.
They didn't know what they didn't know.
Didn't know enough to know what they did want.

So how does the democratic classroom work?
Why would kids try what they weren't good at?
What if a kid never chose math?
What if a kid never chose to read or to write?
How does a teacher balance what kids *want* to know
        and what they *should* know?
I aired my questions in our evening seminars.

"Why," my prof asked, "are you resistant to Dewey?"
"How," I responded, "do you end up educated?
How do you learn about the world?"

With no real answers, my mentor Jon was fine
watching kids learn how they learned. But I
struggled right alongside the flounderers
trying to find my footing—
      my place in the kids' learning
      my place in the classroom
      my philosophy in this newfound field.

Invitations to Real World Questions

I

Teachers' plans, I quickly learned,
come from everywhere.

From Durham's daily news
and city council's concerns,
I asked my troop of Oyster River kids:
"Does our little college town
need a traffic light—
our little town
that rolls up sidewalks
when college students
scatter to the winds
for summer break?"
Jumping at the chance
to investigate,
the kids counted cars
each morning for a week as we stood
at the corner of Madbury and Main.
(Consider today that one traffic light
costs between $80,000 and $500,000
and costs $8000 to run and maintain.)
Without Google for such info,
we must have consulted an almanac.
Wherever and whatever we looked up,
I do recall the kids decided
the answer was no:
Too expensive
Durham did not need a traffic light.

II

The saying goes
that teachers end up teaching
the way they were taught.
If true, that's got to be disheartening
for teacher educators who try so hard
to harness their students' budding dreams
of being different.
More than falling back on how I was taught,
I latched on to how I learned.

And how I learned was often from home projects
not school projects. My father worked
for the Panama Canal Company,
bought supplies for the Canal Zone.
When tasked to find out which grocery store
in the city had the best prices, he asked us for help.
Given a list of products, we went to three stores,
recorded and then compared prices.
It felt clandestine (my father advised us
for whatever reason, to be discrete),
which, of course, made it all the more fun.

I broached the question to my Oyster River crew:
"What grocery store is cheaper?"
"Hannaford," Ben shouted.
"Market Basket," Becky retorted.
"Hannaford."
"Market Basket."
"How," I posed, "could we really find out?"
We devised an oh-so-similar plan

as when I was their age.
Kids were eager to do
math homework.

Benny

Benny was smart
made an intricate model
of an Esso turned Exxon Station
solved any math problem
tinkered with machines.
But, a sixth grader,
he still couldn't read.

I was determined
to be the one
to reach him.
　　Tried Each One Teach One
　　Tried flashcards of sight words
　　Tried phonics
　　Tried writing in sand
　　Tried topics he loved.
Nothing worked.

His father couldn't read either.
Both had dyslexia
(first time I'd heard that word).
Everyone else made peace
with the fact that Benny couldn't read.
I could not.
I chalked it up as a giant failure.

Videotaped

Watching myself
with my professor, John Chaltas,
was torture.
But John was encouraging,
pointing out good things I did.
And I did
kind of look like a teacher
choreographing check-ins
with quiet readers
with pairs about projects
with my group adapting a novel
into a play they'd perform.

But my voice.
Did I really sound like that?

PART III

ELEMENTARY TEACHER

GEORGIA
DACULA ELEMENTARY

The First Week

Newly minted teacher,
first job, first day
and I came home
tired.
No, not just tired—
exhausted.

Early to bed didn't help.
I tossed, turned, my body hot…
I couldn't be sick.
I was never sick, but
I was.
This was my first job,
my first day.
I couldn't stay home.
I didn't.

Fever spiked
in the night
to the point of
hallucinations but still
first-year teacher
went to school.

During recess,
I lay on the classroom rug

my second grade compatriot
watching my kids on the playground.

During lunch,
I napped on the rug
couldn't face food
needed quiet.

I'd been raised
to be responsible.
How could I
have called in sick?

Did I even consider
what I did
was not responsible
to my twenty-two second graders?
I got through it. Somehow.

But I have no real memories
of my first week of my first job.

Beginning Again—And Again

Let's just say I started the year
with twenty-two second graders
in my own little class
until I didn't.

      Seems a new high school was being built
      but not finished and we were in their old building
      (the former elementary site condemned).
      So, the high school start date was delayed
      until they could delay no more.
      And admin had a space crunch.

Soooooo, for half the year
let's just say we started the year again:
with forty-four second graders, two teachers
in a space meant for one class.

We had only a weekend—two novice teachers
to meet, reorganize, and figure out how in hell
to make this work.
With no room for forty-plus desks,
kids and teachers circulated all day:
      reading corner
      phonics center
      writing center
      art center
      math center
      science center
      reading instruction with teacher
We liked to believe it was organized chaos.

Come January, the high schoolers moved
to their now finished building,
and we began again.

Let's just say that I would end the year
with twenty-odd second graders
in my own little class but
what a beginning. . . .

Southern Word Families

"Bell, fell, sell...." I wrote on the blackboard,
pronouncing each word, carefully
enunciating initial and final consonants.
"Who can add to our word family?"
"Way-ell," Judy Muller called out in her
inimitable southern twang.
"W – e – l – l." I spelled out loud
as I wrote, adding the new word to our list.
"Not that kind of *way-ell*," Judy drawled,
"the kind of *whale* that swims in the sea."
Indeed, *well* and *whale* had become homonyms
or is that homophones?

I understood in that moment
my grad professor's skepticism,
his we'll-see response to my dogmatic claims—
I'd seen the light in the reading wars.
I was convinced by the *Why-Johnny-Can't-Read* battle cry:
phonics as the sure-fire route to reading.

Who knew that in rural Georgia
w-e-l-l and *w-h-a-l-e*
nested neatly, at least for Judy,
in a word family.
So much for phonics;
so much for dogmatic beliefs.

Classroom Discipline

I guess we had
role-played bullies
in our grad school seminar
so as newbies we could figure out
how we'd respond.

We had never talked about Carol—
ten years old in second grade
belligerent in words and deeds
so much bigger, taller, chubbier
than seven-year-old second graders.

We had never talked about why bullies bully—
"You know her daddy is in prison,"
teachers whispered behind their hands.
"And her mother—well . . ." their voices petering out,
the shame of her parents plastered on their whispers.

Poor Carol.
I wanted to love her, to hug her.
She had no idea how to be loved
and I
was at a loss.

What Little People Know

While the world swirls around you
and the country's troubles play out
on round-the-clock coverage of
Washington's news, you wonder
what little people know. And so I asked:

"Have you heard of Watergate?
        Not like I expected
        second graders would know
        of the Republican break in
        at Democratic Headquarters,
        of President Nixon's likely role,
        of the little guys taking the fall,
But what *do* little people know?

I pressed them again:
"What do you think Watergate *might* be?"
Veronique, recently moved from France,
 chimed in with her charming accent,
"When the big fishes eat the little fishes?"

She had no idea how right she was.

Unaware

Of course I read to my second graders.
       Every day.
It was our morning ritual (*Stuart Little* was a favorite.)
Of course, I must have read dozens of short books.
       After all, I had fallen in love
       with picture books a couple years before
       in Professor Coleen Salley's "Kiddie Lit"
       class, the summer of '71.

I hope I read the groundbreaking *Snowy Day*
to my southern seven-year-olds who'd never seen snow.
       But it would be decades
       before I noticed the very last page, where
       Ezra Jack Keats' mountains of snow
       flanking the two new friends,
       one white, one Black
       mimicked the map of Africa.

I hope I read *Corduroy* to my all-white class
so they could meet the little Black girl
       who was just like them
       who loved a little stuffed bear
       and helped him find his button.

I hope I read *Little Blue and Little Yellow*
to help my fledgling readers dig deep—
       to see that the story was so much more
       than a blue blob and yellow blob
       befriending one another,
       hugging one another tight

till they blended to green
then being rejected
by their families
who didn't recognize them—
until they cried tears
that dissolved their greenness.

I doubt I did.
I fear I led us all
to thoughtless whiteness.
No doubt, way back when,
I denied us all
a window to the wider world.

Second Grade Play #1

"Ready?" I whispered.
In their places, in The Hundred Acre Wood
Christopher Robin, Winnie, and Eeyore nodded.

Six weeks of rehearsals behind us.
Lines learned, costumes donned.
Parents awaiting in their cafeteria seats.

I pulled the curtain
and Gene stood there, mum,
immune to lines whispered.

I closed the curtain
delivered a pep talk.
Yes. Gene was ready.

Not.

Three times I opened that curtain
Three you-can-do-it talks
before Gene à la Christopher Robin would speak.

Of course, the kids were a hit.

Second Grade Play #2

Cinderella and her stepsisters
had no such fears as the curtain opened
on their own little corner in their own little room.
"Clean, my room!" "Fix my hair!" the stepsisters ordered.

"I want to go to the ball," Cinderella cried. And she did.
Gina and Rodney danced (but wouldn't kiss).
EWWW!
Stepsisters swayed to Strauss waltzes
as only second graders can.

Stage merriment swirled around
the slightly bored Queen Jody
on her throne
picking her nose.

The Last Week

Three "professional days"
after the kids' last day.
Seriously?
What for?
I'd already accepted a transfer
to a new school, moving up to fifth grade.
This first year was finished—
myriad materials hauled home.

Classroom cleaned? Check.
Student grades? Submitted.
Student folders? Completed and filed.

I called in sick
(the only time all year).
"Injured myself hiking in the mountains,"
I told my principal.
Two free days!
Two days not in meetings
I'd deemed irrelevant.

Showed up the very last day—injury on display
Was my arm in a sling?
Was I in an ace bandage and limping?
Was I on crutches?
Who remembers not-real memories?
"Wow, you really were sick,"
fellow teachers said.
"What happened?"

And I regaled them all
about my fictional hiking mishap.

What a difference a year makes
so the saying goes.
Alone in my classroom
I packed first-year mistakes in boxes
ready to start over.

PEACHTREE ELEMENTARY

A Walk in the Woods

Tall, oafy, gangly Nelson
with his too big crooked teeth and
goofy smile—
class clown of Peachtree Elementary.
Not the kid you'd expect
to pen a poem you'd remember
some four decades hence
Not the kid you'd expect
to embrace the essence
of an image capturing haiku's brevity,
not simply counting syllables.
Yet he did.
Here it is:

> *Birds*
> *A band of whistles*
> *led by no one at all*

Nelson would be fifty-six now
I knew him when he was eleven.
I doubt
that he remembers those words
scribbled in the woods behind the school
where we paused for haiku moments.
Doubt he remembers his fifth grade teacher.

But who knows? Memory has
a strange way of immortalizing moments.

Vocabulary Lesson

"Nuisance," I called out.
"Who can make a sentence with 'nuisance'?"
Sherry's hand shot up, but she didn't wait to be called on.
(She had that annoying habit of never waiting to be called on.)
"My brother nuisances me."

Pinched faced Sherry P.
may not have parsed parts of speech,
but she grasped conjugation in grammar.

Blue Eyes Brown Eyes

Co-teachers, Jerri and I peered at our students'
eyes as they filed in from the busses.
"You've got brown eyes.
                                    Sit there.
You're in the low group."
"Blue eyes? Ahh, one of the smart ones.
You can choose where you want to sit."

It took fifteen minutes. Just
as it had for Jane Elliott's class
divided some six years before
the day after Martin Luther King
was assassinated. Ms. Elliott knew
she had to do something to attack prejudice.
She had watched pleasant, sweet children
turn on their peers. We saw the same.

"She's stupid. She has brown eyes,"
chanted a blue-eyed child. "Brown eyes,
brown eyes," several taunted in unison.
"Ha, ha, you don't get recess."
One left the room, claimed
to office personnel he was sick
and needed to go home. Then
another and another. "The teachers
are treating us bad," someone said,
which brought the principal
and an earlier-than-intended debriefing.

"What happened here?" we asked,
 as we ended day one of our experiment.
"What did you learn today?"

Fundraising

Not every fifth grader could afford
the cost of our spring trip to Washington, D.C.
Hence, the events: fish fries, spaghetti dinners,
talent show (faculty included).
Sure, Jerri could sing.
Sure, I could play classical piano.
But polite applause for music kids dislike?
It wasn't our style. Instead, we set up an act:
"Talent Show Auditions"
Jerri sang—mic in hand
belting out lyrics
off-key.
"Next!" the auditioner called.
(Jerri slunk off the stage.)

In my wrinkled, tacky
green velvet gown
I ceremoniously placed
a candelabra on the piano
(Liberace style)
caressed the keys, the familiar strains
of Beethoven's *Moonlight Sonata*—
Messed up
Started over
Messed up
Started over
Third time was *not* the charm
as the auditioner grabbed the candelabra
and chased me off stage.

The laughter of the audience
resounded our success.

Accompanist at the Mall

Nine years of piano lessons
brought me here
dashing through the snow
on a one-horse open sleigh,
playing the jingle bell rock
for our school chorus…

Before there had been professor dreams
before there had been writer dreams
there had been concert pianist dreams
because, for all its terror,
I loved that my piano teacher
picked me at age nine
to play for the big kids' recital.

Ever since sitting in concert halls
hearing the hush fall over the crowd
as lights darkened and the pianist
emerged from back stage,
I'd practiced the slight bow,
taking my seat at our baby grand
(playing not practicing)
picturing those first chords
the rippling sequences
as fingers flew over the keys
to a triumphant close
and thundering applause.

I was never good enough.
Never serious enough.
Never worked enough.
At nine, I'd dreamed of going to Julliard
because I loved its musical name—
Julliard.
At nineteen, I dreamed of giving a senior recital.
I couldn't make it happen,
couldn't memorize the music,
so I quit lessons instead
my senior year in college
just as I had quit lessons
in eighth grade.
I wanted to play and *be* good
Not practice to *get* good.

Philosophy major me
wondered the extent of knowledge
pondered the nature of talent.
If I *did* practice eight hours a day—
could I ever be good enough?
What came first—the desire or the talent?
Had the desire never been
deep enough to develop ability?

I knew, sitting at the piano
amid the Christmas décor at the mall,
it was likely I'd screw up
the chorale of Beethoven's Ninth. But
no one would really notice.
With fake snow clinging to the trees
with bustling shoppers hustling,

with adorable children singing,
at long last, I really was
good enough.

True (Fifth Grade) Love

Something happens
between fall and spring
in fifth grade. . . .
Somehow the young fourth graders
who came to you
in September
just good buddies, just friends
are all paired off
by January.

Michelle and Philip—
arms linked as they strolled ahead of me
on Pennsylvania Avenue in D.C.
"I wish we hadn't met until we were older," Michelle said
with a savvy beyond her eleven years.
"What we have now won't last."

Called to the Office

David was the new kid
moved from California to Georgia.
He. Knew. Everything.
Other kids? Not so much.
"How come David's so smart?"
someone asked.
(Who asks a question like that?)
"Maybe he went to a better school,"
I quipped.

Maybe a kid reported me.
Maybe a parent reported me.
I was summoned to the office
by the principal.
       I perched on the edge of the chair.
       Blood running cold.
       Heart racing.
I can still feel the shame.
(Who says what I said—
about the newest school,
the crown jewel in the county?)

My arrogance exposed—
lesson to learn:
keep my big mouth closed.

Recess

I can picture him—
short in stature, shaggy hair, always in his eyes
crouched at bat like a pro
tapping home plate
ready for the pitch.
Swing!
Connect!
Line drive to shortstop.
(I was shortstop.)

       Teacher crumbling to the ground
       like a bird shot from the sky
       must have momentarily
       blacked out.

When I came to,
a ring of fifth graders
circled me
peering down
faces frightened.
"Are you okay?"

"Looks like I caught that ball
with my mouth," I said
feeling the swelling
feeling fortunate to still have my teeth intact
feeling sorry for the kid.

Can you imagine
how you'd feel
hitting your teacher
in the face?

Fast-forward forty years
to a dentist's office—
I needed crowns for my two front teeth.
"They have internal cracks.
It's as if they were hit," the technician told me.
            "Could have been a long time ago."
"Ahh, yes," I said. "It was,"
and I recalled that day
at recess.

Latent Fears

It was 1979.
Twenty-five years
since Brown v. Board of Education
requiring integration "with all deliberate speed."

Sixteen years since
I, a staunch civil rights advocate,
talked back to my seventh grade gym teacher
who told me, "You don't know the pitfalls of integration."

Ten years since
I had graduated from high school
where only one Black student attended
whom I had befriended (but we never really liked one
another).

Six years since
I had begun my teaching career and worked
in lily-white districts. I could hardly call it chance
that I hadn't sought jobs in now all-Black city schools.

Truth be told, I was
scared of what I never knew, of people I'd never met
scared that I couldn't handle the discipline, as if fights
would be the norm, as if, as if what? What did I really
fear?

With my return
to New Orleans, I applied to teach
at a small private school. Who had I become?

NEW ORLEANS, LOUISIANA
FOREST PARK ELEMENTARY

Scientist Poet

David, at eight
loved science.
Declared his future:
to be a scientist.

He did not
love to write—
until he did.

Something subversive
happened when
I immersed this third grader
in poetry. Copying a poem each day
to practice penmanship,
writing to prompts each week
to explore their voices,
David absorbed
a subliminal missive.

By year's end
the all-science-all-the-time
guy announced:
"When I grow up,
I either want to be
a scientist or a poet."

Made me smile.

Unprepared

If you had asked me
what language they speak in Iran,
I'm embarrassed to say
I could not have told you.
But there she was, Arezoo,
in my third grade.
She spoke only Farsi.

Clueless where to begin,
I returned to each-one-teach-one,
grateful for the materials from college.
I recorded picture books each night
a ping of a spoon on glass—
her signal to turn the page.
Alone at a desk in the back,
bedecked with earphones,
recorder, and my homemade methods,
Arezoo sat, immersed in sounds of English.
Alongside the printed word,
illustrations ushered her
into this oh-so-foreign language
with a different alphabet
as she listened again and again.

There were some tears of frustration,
but mostly she endured isolation during lessons,
endured the remarks about the pungent palate
of her brown bag lunch. "Eww! What's she eating?"

But mostly, her best teachers were her buddies—
the amazing girls
who took her under their wing
and taught her everything.

By year's end,
I had to shush
this once-silent student
who now never stopped talking.

Colonial Day

The long awaited celebration at last arrived.
After months of studying explorers and
months of Plymouth Rock and other early settlers,
after weeks of preparation—
making cardboard Horn Books
readying our slates,
    (in actuality, black construction paper and chalk)
fashioning the dunce cap in the corner,
learning colonial games for recess,
alerting parents of the order of the day:
Corporal punishment would be allowed.

Lights off in the classroom.
Fifty-star flag removed.
In they filed, girls in long skirts,
boys with socks pulled over their uniform pants
à la seventeenth-century breeches.
They faced their stern-faced teacher,
unusually solemn.

A knock at the closed door:
Stephanie was late.
Stephanie—replete with Martha Washington cap
and knapsack lunch in hand.

"You," I intoned harshly, "are late.
Bend over."
Tap tap went my wooden Horn Book on her bum.

Sniveling and scared, Stephanie stood,
her words tumbled out,
"My horse wouldn't start."

It was all I could do to keep a straight face.

Quitting Time

Twice I quit teaching kids.

From the rearview window,
I have trouble saying why.
Maybe it's just this:

Teaching is hard.

If you have thirty students in class,
you carry the load of thirty lives
in your heart
every day.
The "discipline problems"
for lack of a better word
drain your spirit.
You feel you manage behavior
(or try to) more than you teach.
It's the poking, the picking, the taunts.
One more "he looked at me funny,"
and you're ready for the funny farm.
It's the sullenness, apathy, hurt feelings,
and defiance that wear you down.
For all the energy that goes to the few,
days go by when you barely say hello
to the cooperative majority
doing what they're supposed to be doing.

After the first quitting time,
I did substitute teaching, then
taught arts and crafts to adults.

After the second quitting time,
I worked for a newspaper.
Accounts payable and receivable
were enough to send me
back to the classroom.

Special Ed Subbing

After one day in a special ed classroom as a substitute,
I was in high demand—"an actual teacher
instead of a baby sitter," the regular teachers said.
Yet I expect that I learned far more than I taught.

Huddled in his wheelchair, pale, fragile Paul
reminded me of Colin in *The Secret Garden*
when Mary first met him at Misselthwaite Manor.
His whiny "I can't" was his mantra,
making you believe he was too weak to hold a pencil.
"Spoiled rotten," was the assistant teacher's diagnosis.
"His parents do everything for him; they hold him back
far more than his spina bifida."

Aisha wore sunshine on her face.
Begging to walk, she squealed with delight
as I gripped under her arms and swung her legs.
She owned an "I can" mantra
making you believe in the power of the positive.

The able bodied pushed
the ones in wheelchairs to the cafeteria.
At the table, a child with Down syndrome
but a steady hand fed the child with cerebral palsy.
So messy, but so sweet. I wanted to weep.

Then there was Michael.
Propped in his wheelchair,
listing a bit to the right,

his mouth hung open, drooling,
his blank eyes, fixed in a far off gaze.
He never spoke. Simply sat.
Day after day.
Locked in a world
that no one could penetrate.
I wept.

I only wished I had
the strength of spirit
of these special teachers
of these special kids.

LOUISIANA – ST. BERNARD PARISH
ARABI ELEMENTARY

Fears

It happened.
Seven years
into my career
my biggest fear
about becoming a teacher—
a kid threw up in class.

I paled.
Nodded yes, as sweet Angela
volunteered to help the kid.
Thank god, there's always
an Angela.

I remember
in second grade
when Alan threw up
at the Halloween party.
I remember
in tenth grade English
when Mark lost his lunch—
a huge belch
then projectile style.
His desk was right next to mine.

There had been Angelas
those compassionate folks
(that I was not)

to usher the sick one
to the nurse—
to the office—
to the restroom.
My teachers,
who also paled,
lined us up
got us out of the room
away from the smell.

I did the same.

Called to the Office—Again

Report cards submitted.
The principal
read *every* one,
called me to the office
berated me:
"You can't send these home."

Mrs. Viverette's voice was cold.
"You can't tell the e's from the i's."

"Yes, ma'am,"
I said,
my face aflame.

"FIX THEM."

I didn't say it but . . .
I'd tried so hard.
I really had.
It had come to haunt me:
My penmanship
had kept me
off the honor roll
in sixth grade.

Professional Development

Always there were days of planning
how we'd change
        the curriculum,
        the assessments,
        or some other damned thing
        that didn't seem to matter. . . .

"While we're talking about improvement,"
I spoke up (to this all-white faculty at an all-white school),
"Wouldn't it be good if we were models
for our students and spoke standard English?"

        Dead silence

broken by the principal's embarrassed tittering
and some strained comment about how we all
could be more careful. Then without missing
another beat, she took up where she left off.

And I was left to stew . . . but not to say:
        It's not as if I don't
        accept, honor, and
        respect my students'
        language. But still,
        shouldn't we, as teachers,
        expose students
        to the language of power
        so they can choose it
        and use it at will?

This would be an internal battle for me
for years to come, never quite settled,
never quite okay to let go that teachers'
verbs and subjects should agree.

MISSISSIPPI – WEST SIDE ELEMENTARY

Lost and Found

Wailing child in the hall on the first day
drew me from my classroom.
"What's wrong, buddy?"
"I. can't. find. my. classroom," he sniffed
a gulp between each word.
"What's your teacher's name?" I asked.
"I. don't. know," he cried.
"What grade are you in?"
"Second," he said. "No. Third."
Ah, an easy fix, I thought.
We had only two third grade teachers.
"Is she Black or white?" I asked,
knowing I would then know
the teacher's name.
He was not reassured.
He wailed louder,
"I don't know."
I smiled, taking his hand.
"We'll find her."
"Is this young man in your class?" I asked
as we peered into Room 102.
"His class must be next door,"
the white teacher told us.
And it was.

It was 1981, Mississippi
and things there were changing.
This little white child

didn't even remember
his teacher was Black.
This is a story I told and retold
over the years
with wonderment
that children are colorblind.
That is, back in the day,
when I thought colorblind a good thing.

School Magazine Editor

Laura submitted a poem
that cried out for help
words of pain
without hope.
Laura was in my after-school writing club.
I thought I knew her,
sixth grader,
in Mr. Johnson's class,
super smart.
I never saw this pain until now.
These kinds of cries for help
precede suicide, I worried.
This is when you wish
that Mississippi schools had counselors.

"May I see Laura, please?"
I asked Mr. Johnson.
We stepped into the hall,
which, blessedly, was quiet.
"Laura," I said, my voice grave.
"I read your poem."
I paused.
"Do you need to talk?"
"It's not about me," she laughed.
"It's okay if it is," I said.
"We're here to listen."
She laughed again.
"I just wrote what I wrote because
it's the sad kind of poem
you publish."

Like I said.
Super smart.

LOUISIANA
JEFFERSON PARISH –
HAZEL PARK ELEMENTARY

Testing Proctor

Without a homeroom class
my task during test week was proctor—
watching kids as they worked,
heads bent, filling in bubbles,
listening as the teacher,
blissfully ignorant
of her mistake,
read and reiterated
"place" instead of "palace"
blissfully ignorant
of changing meaning
on a listening comprehension test.

I cringed inside
but didn't correct the teacher.
Maybe I helped her save face,
probably helped the kids
get wrong answers.

When Numbers Don't Add Up

We were a couple kids short
of numbers needed for
three fifth grade classrooms.
I had been assigned to teach fifth grade
and prepped all summer.
But as the last hired,
I'd be the first to go.

I pounded the pavement
for kids on the roster
who didn't show:
–One out of state
–One out of district
–One, choosing to stay home
 caring for her newborn baby

She was twelve years old.

My Sister's Garage

Okay, dear readers, I know you're wondering about the
    above title.
Seriously, how does a garage figure into one's teaching life?
I was now a sixth grade teacher (yes, an overnight
    switch—so much
for a summer of planning, but I digress).
None of the sixth grade teachers
wanted to teach science, so the principal made a deal:
Volunteer to teach science and you won't get the low
    reading group.
After three years teaching remedial reading,
I longed for kids who might *like* to read.
I volunteered—despite a dearth of background in science.

Here's the backstory:
When I was in elementary school, teachers let us choose:
Did we want health or science?
(Guess they didn't know science either.)
We chose health, so as Sputnik-era kids,
we were in a black hole of science.
When I was in junior high,
I had a madman who wired his desk
so we would receive shocks if we got too close.
I am not kidding.
High school and college biology: my sum total of science.

Back to the garage:
To teach science you need stuff
and with apartment living, you don't have stuff.
But my sister's garage had oil for viscosity,

bike pumps for air pressure,
little pieces of wood for inclined planes,
soils and seeds for planting…
You get the idea.
Every weekend, my sister and I were a team
trying out the latest science experiment.

Come Monday, I did what I could,
explained best I knew.
I turned most often to
poor brilliant Jason.
I taught him nothing.
He taught the class everything—
explaining his results,
explicating the principles behind the process.
Well done, I would say,
hoping he was right.

The Understudy

When "bad kids" are absent
which they almost never are
(makes sense, their mamas
want them out of the house too)
the heart takes a little leap.

That one brief moment of realization—
the kid's empty desk—
is just that.
Brief.

Waiting in the wings
another troublemaker surfaces
and takes center stage.

Imagined Future Revisited

My being-a-professor dream
from way back when
wasn't really real
for the philosophy-major-me.
What would I profess?
In fact, the being-professor
dream lay dormant for years.

As I crept, one course at a time,
for ten years toward my doctorate,
(I had tenure as a student
before a tenure track job)
I resented college professors
who had taught kids for only four years—
only four months in one case.
They rarely had real answers
to my questions for how to reach
hard-to-teach kids
how to teach
hard-to-reach kids.

But they did teach me this:
When I got good enough
as a teaching-kids-me,
I wanted to teach teachers.
        I had a ways to go.

ABCs of Teaching

All-consuming,
both banal and
creative, teaching
demands dedication.
Every kid's
feelings
give a
harbinger, an
inkling, of
just the
kind of day you're
likely to have. If kids are
manic,
non plussed,
or
pissed off, you
quickly
realize the
sort of day
today will *not* be:
uneventful.
Visions vanish of
willing students
'xpecting
you to
zealously engage them.

CLANCY ELEMENTARY

Real World Connections

My position: Title I teacher for reading and math.
My students: Low scorers with low skills
in desperate need to see connections
between the real world
and the subjects they failed ...

Who doesn't love receiving letters?
We painted liquor boxes—strong sturdy cartons
with partitions—and created mailboxes.
Each kid had a turn to be the mail carrier,
sorting daily missives we wrote to one another.
(Yes, this was way before email and texting.)
Just about the time the cartons sagged,
just about the time that newness wore off,
we needed another project.

Who doesn't hate litter?
We gathered litter in the schoolyard:
  homework papers gone awry,
   gum and candy wrappers on the fly,
   cups and napkins landing from nearby.
We sorted it, counted it, analyzed its source
finding the worst culprit to be fast food.
We penned, practiced, and performed
for a school assembly
skits that spread our anti-litter campaign.

Resistant Readers

My troop of Title I students
struggled with spelling
wrestled with writing
resisted reading
with every excuse they could muster.
Today the teacher in the next room
was especially loud.
My students sighed,
put heads on their desks.
"How can we concentrate?"
they implored to no avail.

Our neighbor teacher
carried on:
"Give me a 'd' word."
"Dad," a kid called out.
"Give me an 'f' word."

'Twas just the levity we needed.

Sobering Moments

It was 10:39 a.m.
January 28, 1986.
Outside my classroom
the principal wept
as she spread the news
of the Challenger
space disaster.
Our little world exploded
with Christa McAuliffe.
She was one of us
            a teacher.

When disasters hit
close to home
they hit harder.

Come Spring

As the school year wore down,
wilted kids blossomed
with my plan to plant a vegetable garden.
"Let's plant tomatoes!"
"Let's plant pumpkins!"
"Let's plant watermelons!"

With each suggestion, I questioned:
"Is that a spring crop?"
They poured over books, garden catalogs,
guides to Louisiana planting.
Voila, they found their crop.
"Can we harvest before the school year ends?" I asked.
"We can plant by March 15," they declared.
"And we'll harvest by May," they calculated.

"What do plants need?" We checked the sun.
"Where will we plant?" We checked a water source.
Opting for a treeless spot nearest the restrooms
(closer to haul buckets),
we measured and mapped
so each kid had a personal plot.

Weekend volunteers helped till the soil,
shake clumps of grass, smooth our spot.
Come Monday, eager gardeners
planted seeds
watered
waited.

Healthy competition ensued:
Whose seeds would first break the soil,
whose two tiny leaves would branch to four,
whose tendrils would reach highest
on the fence as we graphed the growth?

Come May, proud gardeners bestowed
the most popular teachers
with piles of cucumbers.

WASHINGTON ELEMENTARY

Sloppy Copy

Angelica's story made no sense.
But how could I say that
without saying that?

Surely, if I read it to her
realization would dawn.
"So how did it sound?" I asked.

She looked at me,
her round eyes wide and glowing.
"Perfect," she said.

And so it was.

Scrooge

Okay, I confess. I really hated
the weeks between Thanksgiving
and Christmas, when kids had nothing
on their minds but impending holidays and presents.
Again, my childhood came to the rescue;
I'd loved leafing through Sears, Roebuck catalogs.

Now, armed with ads and catalogs (no internet yet),
I devised our math curriculum: priorities and empathy.
"If you could choose what you wanted
what would you put on your Christmas list?"
The greedier they were, the more they had to add.
They did it: LONG math problems. No problem.

"What if you could choose just five things?"
"What if your family's budget was $200.00
for all members of the family?"
"What if *your* budget was $20.00
to buy presents for everybody?"
"What's more important—the getting or the giving?"

Teacher Evaluation

Clipboard in hand, Principal Evangeline
slipped into my remedial reading class:
Five kids worked on fluency
with some newfangled reading machine.
Three sprawled on the carpet reading.
Others gathered in the writing corner,
scribbling, staring into space,
scribbling a little more.

I waltzed from group to group guiding,
conferring, tending to fickle technology.
Evangeline tapped me on the shoulder
announcing in a too loud whisper:
"I'll come back
when you're teaching."

Cross-grade Tutoring

Problem: Fifth and sixth graders reading at a second
  grade level.
Where does one begin?
     They can't read because they don't read.
     They don't read because they can't read.
Who wants to do something you're not good at?
Who wants to read books for little kids
when you're a big kid?

Solution:
Give them a reason to read on their level.
So was born our cross-grade tutoring project.
Who wants to appear foolish to a five year old?

Triumph:
Remedial readers now practiced fluency and expression
because they had an adoring audience.
With the stigma of "baby books" removed,
they came to the reading lab
(even at recess) to plan their lessons.

"Fond Memories"

You've gotta love
when a sixth grader drops by
before she graduates to middle school
clutching the book to her chest
that she had written three years before.
"I still have my book," she says.
She pauses and tells you with a sigh,
"I have such fond memories
of this classroom."
(I hoped it was more than fond memories of the space—
the cute cat curtains at the windows
the carpeted reading corner surrounded by bookshelves.)

I hoped, maybe,
she had fond memories
of the community
of readers and writers
we'd become in this place.

BARBRE JUNIOR HIGH

Involuntarily Transferred

Fresh with Ph.D. initials after my name,
I was involuntarily transferred
to Barbre Junior High.
Here are the stats:
Five classes of reading
One class of Spanish
153 students
45% in seventh grade for the second time
15% in seventh grade for the third time

Here's the scenario:
Teaching without my own room
Not enough desks for each kid on the roster
No shelves for YA books to prove
that they could like to read.

At least they liked freewrites
that began each day.

As I lugged thirty composition books
into the teacher's lounge
Mr. Smith shook his head.
"You're like a new teacher," he said.
"How long you been teaching?"

Routinely, he regaled us with his stats:
"Eight months, twenty-four days till I retire."
"Eight months, twenty-three days...."
"Eight months, twenty-two days...."
(Who knew he'd outlast me?
I would give notice soon after.
Wouldn't even last eight weeks.)

Control

Middle-school discipline 101
eluded me as I tried
to corral control.
        Couldn't wait them out.
        They didn't care.
        Raised my voice.
        The din died down
just long enough for
Justin to intone:
"My dad said we'd better
listen to her. She's a doctor."
(I think he felt sorry for me.)
"Ooooooh," several chorused.

I could hear the students'
unsaid aside:
Big fucking deal.

Melee

"Fight, fight, fight,"
several students chanted.
I hadn't seen it start,
wouldn't see it end
as I was knocked to the floor
trying to intervene.
I hadn't gotten a Ph.D. for this.

Tears

Cried every day driving home
Rallied by morning with new plans
Dashed by third period.

Maybe

Maybe it wasn't just me.
Months later,
after I'd quit and moved on,
I found out this seventh
grade crew went through
five teachers that year.

Why didn't that make me
feel better? Anyone can teach
good motivated kids.
What kind of teacher was I
if I couldn't reach the hard to teach?

A Father's Critique

"Why are you always changing jobs?"
my father often asked me.
My father who had started
sweeping floors and stayed
with the same company
until he was top boss.

My father who pegged me
for the business world.
(Where that came from I'll never know.)
"I'm not changing jobs," I'd tell him.
"I'm still a teacher,
looking for the perfect fit."

Fifteen Year Slump

Like many teachers, I started my career
wanting to change the world.
Like many teachers, I had dreams
to make learning what it hadn't been for me.

I'd read once that Helen Keller said
school interrupted her learning.
Was I creating a classroom that did that?
Somewhere along the line I'd lost my fire.

Woke up one day and knew
I had succumbed to too many worksheets.
I was no longer changing the world at all.
Surrounded by mediocrity, I had joined it.

BACK TO GRAD SCHOOL

First Impressions

When I first met Professor Bud
I hated him.
I wish I could recall the icebreaker
that raised my hackles
first night of first class
pigeonholing him
as a footnote to the sixties.
And I wasn't feeling it.

Just out of school, and here I was
back again (post-doc) considering
certification to teach gifted kids.
It may have seemed a good idea
at the time but I dropped the class.

Big mistake.

A couple months later, with job in hand
teaching gifted students, I had to beg
Dr. Bud to let me enroll
in the next course
next semester
sans prerequisite.

He resisted
but acquiesced.

Second Impressions

"Teaching is about relationships,"
Bud said to the class.
"I can be your teacher if you let me."
And that was it.
I was like a cicada emerging
from underground.

Something stirred, simmered,
stoked a fire that had grown cold.
      Provocative readings
      thoughtful assignments
      rich discussions
brought me full circle
to philosophy and how we learn
full circle to the ideas and ideals sparked
by John and Jon in New Hampshire
at the start of it all seventeen years before.

Bud was a listener. Quiet. Intense.
Interjecting just the right question
at just the right time to trigger
more talk that he could take in.

Listening. Quiet. Intense.
When he spoke, he
wound everyone's words
and the week's readings
to reawaken in us all
why we wanted to teach.

To say he created a community
of learners, which he did,
does not capture
the experience that fueled me
for the next seventeen years.

LOUISIANA – ORLEANS PARISH
Teacher of the Gifted and Talented

Teacher Evaluation that Matters

In my first week in my new gig
with gifted students
we carved out a community
in our closet classroom.
(Literally, we were housed
in a five-foot-by-eight-foot space,
once a cloak room of what became the library.)

Sometimes, when no classes
were scheduled for library time,
we sought larger spaces.
Tables became ours for projects.

As we carved out pumpkins
and penned Halloween poems,
eight-year-old Tasha turned to me,
a wise serious look on her face,
"You're good with children,"
she said and smiled.

Itinerant Teacher

If it was Tuesday, it must be Moton,
me and one sprite six year old, Kierra
at least for a few months or so—
long enough to develop a rapport
long enough for projects and trust
before some power-that-be
yanked me from Moton
(Why, I wanted to know
but received no answer.)
Assigned me to Phillips Jr. High.

I'll never know what transpired
with Moton's new teacher,
never learned the back story
only that I was reassigned
(yanked from Phillips after just
long enough to develop a rapport
long enough to trust and start projects)
I was again at Moton
at the principal's demand:
        "Get me that white lady back."

SHAW ELEMENTARY

Writing Conference

"Once upon a time," Tasha typed,
intent as she gazed at the computer.
I wasn't surprised to see her
writing a fairy tale.
She loved fairy tales.
Read from one end of the 398.2 shelf
to the other. Even knew the Dewey number
that housed her favorite stories.

(Her life was not a fairy tale.)

She penned her princess
with blue eyes and long blond hair.
"Why," I asked, as I peered at the screen,
"is your princess blond?"

"All princesses are blond,"
came her don't-you-know-anything sassy quip.

"Why isn't your princess Black?" I asked.

With an unbelieving question mark
in her voice, her head cocked
in inimitable-Tasha-style,
"She can be?"

Mirrors

For our newly formed book club,
Tasha picked out Mildred Taylor's *The Friendship*.
Choosing to stay in at recess to read,
she smiled up her light-up-the-world smile
as she read aloud:

> *"Now don't y'all go touchin' nothin'," Stacy warned.*
> *"And Cassie, don't you say nothin'."*
> *"Now, boy, what I'm gonna say?"*
> *"Just mind my words, hear?"*

Tasha twirled around the room
chanting the lines over and over

> *"And Cassie, don't you say nothin'."*
> *"Now, boy, what I'm gonna say?"*

She'd never before
seen her language in a book.

Untitled

When Tasha returned to school
after her uncle killed her father
no one knew what to say or do.

Tasha stared at the blackbird
preserved in alcohol
in our science corner.

"He doesn't hurt anymore, does he?"
"No, Tasha," I said. "He doesn't."
That, and a hug, was enough.

Dealing with Daryl

It wasn't long before endearing Daryl
     my inveterate reader
     my lover of facts
     inhaler of books
was no longer endearing.

(Think having Charles Manson
in your class as a fourth grader.)
He was unquestionably gifted
unquestionably defiant
denied hurting others,
defied accusations of stealing
was, in fact, devoid of empathy.

Looking for answers
I read *High Risk: Children
Without A Conscience*
And there was Daryl
on the pages:
Superficially charming
Exploiting others
Chilling and unrepentant.

Path to Perfect Poems

Janae was on fire
writing poems about ballet
cranking out poem
after en pointe poem
with forced rhymes.
Her friends, her family,
her classroom teacher
lavished her with praise.

My gifted kids were smart,
used to praise.
They were not
used to critique.
"Try free verse," I suggested.
"These rhymes sacrifice
sense for sound."

Always quiet,
always perfect Janae
threw down her paper,
indignantly
raising her voice:
"Everyone else
loves my writing.
But when I show my poems to you,
you always criticize them."
    Her eyes, her tone
    sent darts into
    my teaching heart.

"Whoa! The last thing I want
is to discourage you.
Critique isn't criticism; it's how we grow.
No writer writes it right
from the start.
Take some time, and then
let's look again at those rhymes."

Epilogue:
Three weeks later
at our publishing party
Janae held to her chest,
illustrated in pastels
bound in her very own book
her now perfect poems.

Instant Poetry

We wrote—all of us—inspired
by pretty papers spread on our writing table:
Silhouetted trees in gradients of green,
an eagle barely there on a palette of blue
fluffy clouds, rainbow streaked.

"Ready? Two minutes," I'd say.
Images before us ignited memories
suggested sounds
that spilled unbidden on the page.

Was it the adrenaline rush of the two-minute deadline?
Was it the communal courage of seven writers
writing without risk?
Turned out we sometimes
churned out poems we liked.

Megan

Even among the gifted,
there are gifted.
Megan was one of those.
Her voice held a hint of mischief;

her eyes shone her brilliance.
At six, she read at a twelfth-grade level.
But in her regular first grade class
she read about Spot and Tuffy.

At six, she was ready for our Equations team.
But in her regular math class
instead of writing from 1 to 100,
her challenge was to write from 100 to 1.

Once classified as GT,
at least for two hours
three days a week
she could fly. . . .

Building Lego castles,
trekking west with Carmen San Diego,
writing books. Proudly, she showed
her handbound book replete with a mylar cover

to her regular teacher
who had to be convinced
it wasn't a book
from the library.

Thumbprint Art

B. J. didn't have just purple thumbs.
Oh, no. B. J. was truly invested
in our newest art project
anointing every finger
as we illustrated poems.

Oh, no! The ink, we discovered,
was indelible.
Too bad that the very next day
(his sister Lynska had not warned me)
B. J. was to be ring bearer
in a family wedding.
White suit.
Purple fingers.

Mama was not pleased.

Some twenty years hence
came a voice from the past:

I would like to believe that you will remember us as vividly and easily as we remember you. We were going through my mom's old papers and discovered several documents written to her by you. We just wanted to take an opportunity to reach out and tell you thank you for investing in us in our younger years.
Love, Lynska and BJ

Maybe Mama hadn't held a grudge after all.

Sometimes You Just Don't Know

I worried
about Jennifer G.
She was shy and quiet
(just like me as a kid).
We seemed a mismatch—
my too effusive, too enthusiastic,
over-the-top teaching
too much for this gentle,
compassionate, inward soul.

Almost twenty years later
a not-familiar student
sought me out at the university.
"Are you Dr. Austin?"
Turned out to be
none other than Jennifer G.
"You are the reason
I became a teacher," she said.

I misread our relationship
all those years ago and told her so.
And I retold the story a few years later
as I introduced Dr. Jennifer
to my multicultural class
to speak about her research
on the school-to-prison pipeline.
> Teacher
> Counselor
> Principal
I needn't have worried
about Jennifer G.

A Treasure Trove

When mysterious algorithms
detect a match and invite you to link in,
I discovered Jennifer G. is now a professor,
reached out to congratulate her,
connected, and heard back.

Dr. Austin!!
Yes, I made the leap into higher ed 4 years ago. I'm still very shy
but tend to push past it when I know there's a greater cause. I
only wish every child in that school had a teacher like you. So
many don't and their life trajectories are so different.

Every teacher has a treasured trove
of notes stashed in a box,
of emails saved in a special file,
reminders, on those bad days,
that teaching-lives
matter.

Just Tired

We read about Rosa Parks
trying to explode the myth
that she was just tired
when she refused to stand up.
        Tired of injustice, yes.

We read about Martin Luther King
parsing his words about the content
of our character.
We read about sit-ins
at lunch counters.

"Do we hafta read one more book
about civil rights?" Craig asked
exasperation in every word.
"We're free now.
Everyone's equal," he said.

"Really?" I responded.
"Do you go to an integrated school?"
Craig shrugged.
"White children *could* go here,"
I added, "but they don't."
He shrugged again—
not convinced
still unwilling to discuss civil rights.

Why was I too blind to see?
Black kids of the nineties
needed today's heroes,
today's victories.
Studying oppression
was oppressive.
Craig was just tired.

What's Wrong With This Picture?

Picture the world's biggest grocery store
but instead of food
books—aisles & aisles & aisles of them.

Picture the movie lover's
chance to attend
Academy Awards.

Such was the scene
at the American Library Association's
convention hall.

Picture frenzied
delirious
bibliophiles

awaiting the day
awaiting the announcement
of this year's awards.

Which books would rise
to win the Newbery, Caldecott,
Coretta Scott King, and Pura Belpré Awards?

Picture the very morning,
the very chance
to be among the first to know.

I spy my school's librarian—
yes, the librarian whose
closet is my classroom.

I shout with glee.
"Are you heading
to the award announcements?"

With a dismissive
shake of her head, she replied:
"Pat and her books."

HARDIN ELEMENTARY

Bested

Sure Dominique and Sarah
were gifted, but they were
      only seven
with astounding fonts of knowledge.

"How," I asked, "do you *know* so much?"
With glints in their eyes
and you're-not-going-to-approve grins,
they responded in tandem,
      "TV."

Self-Censoring

Sarah, at nine, was developing.
So I recommended the book
Are You There, God? It's Me, Margaret.
"I love Judy Blume," Sarah said,
happily plunging into its pages.

It wasn't long before, wide-eyed,
she handed the book back
with a shake of her head.
"I'm not ready for this."

Phone Conversations

One of my great failings:
        keeping connected
to those over the years
who have meant so much to me.
One great gift:
those who kept up with me.
Sarah was one.
On occasional phone calls during her high school days
I loved hearing about her interests, her projects
        (loved that she was researching Leontyne Price).
I loved telling her when she graduated,
        how proud her dad would be.
(She carried his photo, she said, tucked in graduation garb.)
I loved hearing where she'd head to college
        that she was headed to grad school
        that she was happily married.

In one assignment, when Sarah was eight,
I must have asked: What do you want to be?
Tucked in memorabilia, safe in my office, are her words:
"I have no idea what I want to be
when I grow up but I hope I'll be a professional."

And indeed she is. For seven years,
together at the university, me as prof,
Sarah in administration,
we reconnected with hugs on graduation days
telling anyone who'd listen our proud connection:
I was her teacher way back when—
till she was ten.

When she moved on, she wrote:

Hi, Doc,
I'm so glad that we were able to reconnect during my time here.
I am still standing on your shoulders as you were a cornerstone
of my education and foundation as a professional.

I couldn't be prouder
to have played a part.

PALMER ELEMENTARY

Ashton

"I'm not finished yet,"
Ashton declared, an annoyed edge
to his voice, as I turned
the page of a picture book.
Silly me, who thought only of words.
Ashton needed more time
to read pictures.

Fast-forward twenty-five years:
Almost zoned out at UNO's graduation,
I hear his name: Ashton S.
B.A. in Business.
I bolted from my seat
to give him a hug
from the past.
I love having completed pictures.

NOMA

They were primped, pumped, and ready
for the New Orleans Museum of Art—
my Palmer crew of five. . . .

For four weeks,
        we explored
        cave paintings of Lascaux,
        crafted our own cave images
        with Conté crayons
        on rough manila paper.

        We sharpened understanding of shape
        as we painted portraits
        of each other, of ourselves,
        all angular features visible at once,
        our own version of cubism.

        We curated colors as we painted
        cerulean people, cyan cats,
        lapis lazuli houses, stark against
        azure skies and turquoise trees—
        a palette of Picasso.

For forty minutes
in the very first room
at the museum, I was proud.
My gifted troop took in every detail,
amazed by the dead rabbits in the still life paintings
amazed by brushstrokes, by colors of Flemish art.

But interest flagged quickly.
Room by room their complaints grew louder,
the marble floors hard and tiring,
the promise of a picnic at Storyland enticing.
Only Ashton, map in hand, wanted to soldier on.

CARVER JUNIOR HIGH

Earning Respect

Resentment from fellow faculty
was intense my first year at Carver.
"Hmmm. Hmmm."
"Only white teacher,
how you get the cream of the crop?"

I was, after all, the teacher
whose students designed board games
about the presidents, who put on a play
about the signing of the constitution.
(Picture Wayne bedecked with a powdered wig.
We foreshadowed *Hamilton*!)
We parsed and analyzed rap lyrics.
"Are you sure?" my trio cautioned protectively.
"The language is pretty rough."
We wrote narratives and poems
and made books. Who wouldn't envy this?

"You back?" some teachers asked
at the start of my second year,
conditioned as they were to the revolving
door for any white teacher assigned there.
Then came the September 1990 teachers' strike.

Who knew that crossing the picket line
would earn me more respect?
"I'm supporting myself," I said.
"I can't afford to be without a paycheck."
"You go, girl. Same here."

Stereotypes

"If you won a million dollars in the lottery
  what would you do?" Wayne asked.
"Probably give it to the SPCA," I said.
"Would you quit your job?"
"And leave you guys?" I quipped. "No way."

"What'd I tell you?"
Wayne turned to his buddies
"I knew she'd say something like that.
All the Black people we asked
  would buy a mansion, a car,
  and quit they jobs."

"Wayne," I said, "you're falling prey
  to negative stereotypes.
You think
  that just because you survey one white
  crazy cat lady that you know
  what all white people would do?"

Students To My Defense

"Why you behave for that white lady?"
the regular English teacher hollered
at my gifted kids.
"She has a name," Charmaine retorted.

Writing Conference

When Wayne handed me
the draft of his story,
something was hidden
in his eyes that I couldn't read.

When I read the story,
I knew his intent: shock value.
The genre had been the students' choice.
Eighth-grade Wayne's selection? Steamy romance.

He waited, I am sure, with bated breath.
Watched me, I am sure, for my reaction.

"Why would you write this?
Why would you write
her creamy white breasts?
Why white?"

His revision was instant:
Her creamy mocha breasts.

Questions Deserve Answers

"With Mrs. Francois, I could figure it out,"
Wayne said. "She has two kids.
Same with Mrs. Washington. She's got
five kids. But you don't have kids."
    If you knew Wayne, you knew
    where this was going. Sure enough,
    he dared to ask the question:
"Have you ever had sex?"

    The most reasonable response
    would have been a rebuke—
    that such a question was
    inappropriate.
    But what message does that send?
    Don't questions
    deserve answers?
"I was married," I said.

That was all Wayne needed
before falling to the floor,
frenzied, howling with laughter.

Leaving

It wasn't easy telling my Carver kids
I wouldn't be returning come fall.
"I'll be teaching at the university," I said.
Clinging as they did to stereotypical images
of white-haired professors
they promptly told me,
"You're not old enough."

Chance Meeting

"Dr. Austin?" said this super tall guy
some fifteen years later, on the university campus.
"Do you remember me?"
He lowered his shades and then I knew.
"Wayne!" I said. "Of course, I remember you.
We had some great times at Carver."

"Oh, yes, we did," Wayne replied,
a broad knowing grin spreading
across his face. "I remember *EVERYTHING*."

PART IV

COLLEGE TEACHER

Adjunct Professor at University of New Orleans

Reflecting

I wondered aloud to Anita,
as together we reflected about reflecting.
"The only students who get it
are deep thinkers, like you,
who had it to begin with.

What, then, does that say about
teaching reflective practice?
What does that say
about teaching, period?"
We didn't have an answer.

TULANE UNIVERSITY

Something's Up

It was eerily quiet
as I headed up the steep stairs
of the Newcomb Nursery Center
past the children's books in the attic room
one more turn to the corner classroom.
This place had been our haven to explore
secret gardens and islands where
blue dolphins swam, where we stood
in awe of the owl moon,
where we were touched by possum magic.
And we got the lowdown,
the true story,
of those wily little pigs.
Last class days are bittersweet.

No students trudged up with me
in a rush to be there on time.
No sound came from the classroom
till I opened the door
to applause as they rose to their feet
and sang a rousing chorus.
For she's a jolly good teacher
For she's a jolly good teacher
For she's a jolly good teacher
which nobody can deny.

Dare I say, I was
speechless,

eyes glistening with tears.
It was, for sure, the only standing ovation
I ever received.

Power in a Name

Two years at Tulane
whose prestige was my gateway
to my coveted job.

Dear UNO Search Committee

I know some members
of the faculty are dead
set against hiring
your own graduates,
that you want
new blood,
new ideas.

I took them on
challenged their argument
before they could confront me
face to face
in the interview.
(Maybe it worked.)

What Ifs

Could have taught gifted kids
so many years before.
The interview with St. Charles Parish
went well, the head honcho eager to hire me.
But I wasn't certified
and didn't get the job.

Could have taught third grade
at a posh private school
whose philosophy seemed in sync with mine.
Were they threatened by the Ph.D.?
What did I do wrong?
Why didn't I get that job?

Applied to teach college
years before, but got
an oh-so-snide response
from Southern University's
English Department Chair
"Why would you get a Ph.D. in *Education?*"

What if any of those paths
had panned out?
They would have led me
someplace else.
I might not have ended up
where I belonged most.
Reason enough to believe in fate.

UNIVERSITY OF NEW ORLEANS
Professor of Children's Literature

Publish or Perish

I don't recall when I first heard
of the looming threat over the academy:
publish or perish.
Perhaps it was dinner table conversation—
my father talking about his professor brother.
I had long known it was a thing.
So why was I surprised at my interview
to be asked my research agenda?

Twenty years as a classroom teacher,
the Tulane job, grant-funded
with no expectation to publish.
Truth be told:
I had no agenda.
But I made one up—fast.
And got the job.

No one needed to tell me the rules.
No one needed to badger me.
If I was on a ladder,
I'd climb rather than fall.
Looked for calls for manuscripts,
learned the journals
set to work:
Top-tier journals
Middle-level national journals
State journals.

I wrote about books,
interviewed authors and illustrators,
wrote about their creative processes,
wrote about trends in the field.
In four years, I climbed the first rung
of the academic ladder.
Five more years, climbed the next rung.

In two dozen years in the hallowed halls,
I watched four colleagues perish.
I owe a hindsight thank you to my parents
who so subtly, so quietly modeled
the drive it takes to succeed in the Ivory Tower.

Math 101 of a Professor's Life
An Outsider's View

I know from my nine-to-fiver father
how hard it is for an outsider
to have an insider view of what you do
as a member of the academy.

"You teach (pause) *how many* classes?" Daddy asked.
"Three," I answered.
"And *how long* (pause) are those classes?"
"I have two courses that meet seventy-five minutes
 twice a week, and my night course is three hours, but . . ."
"That means," he interrupted
        (I aptly guessed where he was going
        with this line of questioning.)
"That means," he reiterated,
"You work nine hours a week."

I was not sure he'd get beyond the "but."
But I did try to explain:
"Work isn't simply the nine hours
you stand before a class.
There are hours of prep, hours of reading, hours
of responding to and grading students' papers, and that's just
the teaching part; the academy expects service on committees
expects research and publishing and . . ."
"Theoretically," he interrupted again
(slicing off my run-on sentence)
"You work nine hours a week."

Sigh.

Math 102 of a Professor's Life
The Inside Story

Average sixty-hour workweeks
S t r e t c h e d   o f t e n
to eighty.
Teaching—just a third of professorial life
amidst meetings—
endless.
Amidst a host of other gerunds:
>   Researching
>   Interviewing
>   Reviewing
>   Writing
>   Observing
>   Conferring
>   Advising
>   Class-prepping
>   Course-administering
>   Laboring over accreditation reports
>   Grading
>   Responding to student work
(And students deserved thoughtful feedback)
Endless.

The magic drudgery of molding critical thought.

Big Shoes to Fill

I had memories of my mentor—
memories of falling in love
with children's books
in the summer of 1971.
Day after day we listened,
enraptured, to stories by Leo Lionni,
Ezra Jack Keats, and Tomie dePaola,
their words drenched in the drawl
of my professor, Coleen Salley.
I earned my Ph.D. to become her,
held my foot in the door
till the opening came at her retirement.

Many things would change.
I was not the French Quarter character—
Krewe of Coleen, whose students
pushed their soused professor
in a grocery cart each Mardi Gras.
I was not the raconteur who could hold forth,
cigarette ash ready to drop
as rapt audiences clung to every word.
I would not shock students
with strings of four-letter words.
And I wouldn't call the course "Kiddie Lit."

Some things would not change
Just as Ms. Salley had,
I read each day from *Charlotte's Web*.

And just as Ms. Salley's did for thirty years,
my voice cracked and tears slid down my face
when Charlotte died.

After class, my most reluctant reader
spoke up: "When you cried,"
she said, "I knew that book
was about more than a pig and spider."
Maybe, just maybe,
I was filling those big shoes.

Charting Paths

Before a semester starts
I am a geographer
mapping a syllabus—
    concepts to teach
    genres to include
    novels to choose
    diversity to balance
    standards to match
    strategies to put in place.
These were my puzzle pieces.
I tinker and worry
think and wonder.
But planning is just planning.
At semester's start,
one huge piece is missing.

During semesters
I am an explorer
using my map
alongside my students
discovering some routes
easy to follow, finding
others require maneuvering
around obstacles, doubling
back, starting over
as I chart myriad paths
to lead future teachers

from being readers
      or not
from being writers
      or not
to a place of comfort
to a place of knowing
that they too can reach
their future students.

At semester's end
I look at all they learned
      about literature
      about life
at all I've learned
      about them
      through them
And my heart is full.

Deep Inside

Each day, I lived my dream job.
Each evening, I lived my worst nightmare.
    I was losing
    my mother
    one memory
    at a time.
"Where are you working?"

        "I teach at UNO now."

"Oh. Right. I knew that."

        "Just think, you were
        working in the UNO
        library twenty-five years ago."

"Really?"

        "Yup. Changing the
        cataloging from Dewey to
        Library of Congress."

"I did that?"

        "Your handwriting in every
        book proves it!
        Makes me smile every time
        I see it."

"Where are you working?"

Deep inside still was the wit—
my mother who wrote funny notes
instead of nagging.
"Know what these are?"
(Picture drawings of tiny clothes hangers
with two stick figures hanging from them.)
"Well use them!"

173

Deep inside still was the maker of story magic.
Hear the cackling witches in fairy tales,
the intonation of the Jewish grandmother—oy vey.
The French Grandpa in *The Family Under the Bridge*. Oooh-la-la.

Deep inside still was Mozart's Sonata in C
that lulled us to sleep as she played piano late at night,
her *Pearl Fishers'* bass to my treble in duets.
(We laughed as much as we played.)

Deep inside still was every kid's favorite camp leader.
Volunteer at Head Start. My fair lady of musical theater,
Le Petit Theatre's backstage award, named in her honor,
Always quick one-liners, kept everyone laughing.

Deep inside still the most perfect person in the universe
who never really believed how absolutely perfect she was.
Though once she'd said, "I can't imagine the world without me."
I couldn't either.

One night that I didn't visit,
she asked my sister, "Where's Pat?"
First time in months she'd said my name.

Each night during visits, my mother knew
she was with someone who loved her
even when she didn't know who I was.

Apology Poem
(with apologies to William Carlos Williams)

This is just to say
I know I have asked you
to read and review
one hundred books
in fifteen weeks
which you have probably
never done in your life.

Forgive me
but they're all
written at a fourth
grade level or less,
and I know you'll love them.

Overworked Student
(or, I Earn a New Name)

Future librarian Bette loved to read
But
one hundred books for Children's Lit?
And
two novels a week in my colleague's
Young Adult Lit course?
All in one semester?
Too much!

Bette dubbed one of us
wicked witch of the east
and the other
wicked witch of the west.

Overdue Book

Jamie had a ten-year-old—
a curious ten year old
with lots of hard-to-answer questions.
What better tool than a book?
When Jamie checked out
Growing Up: It's a Girl Thing,
it lived under her daughter's bed
the whole semester.

When Jamie finally returned the book
she sheepishly shared
that every girl in her neighborhood
had visited her daughter's room
had learned everything
they didn't know
they wanted to know.

I had hoped my role
teaching teachers would
widen my ripples of influence.
Never in my wildest wonderings
did I imagine how teaching teachers
might also be teaching parents
might lead to sexual awakening of a bevy of girls
from a bucolic bedroom community.
Who knew?

Shared Stories

When you teach
teachers, you share
so many similar passions,
so many similar stories.

I read a lot.
Barbara, even more.
Needless to say,
we bonded over books.
She reads hundreds of books,
thousands of books,
millions and billions,
and trillions of books.
(Thank you, Wanda Gag).

How could I resist
the borrowed hyperbole?
We laughed (and despaired)
over stories
of inept administrators.
One principal asked to observe her
when she was teaching
hyper-bowl.

We bonded, too,
when our teaching lives
followed parallel plotlines.
Remember this, readers.
It is foreshadowing.

Two Roads Converged

Fellow children of the fifties
following different paths
for decades, now we meet:
Marilyn, mother of four,
lived life on the road
with her traveling musician.
I, mother of cats,
lived life in classrooms.
Yet, we immediately bonded.
"I'd always wanted to be a teacher
but Spencer's art came first," Marilyn said.
"I'd always wanted to be a children's author
but I sabotaged my own art
by never making time to write."
"Oh no," Marilyn said. "Your art
is teaching. I watch what you do.
After that student read aloud today,
            mispronouncing words,
            stumbling over sentences,
            missing punctuation,
            reading without expression,
            practically near tears—
you saved face for her, praising
her book choice."

Our roads intersected,
Marilyn's and mine,
the summer
my picture book was published.
(What if I'd given to writing

all the time I'd given to teaching?
Might I have many more books
with my name on the spine
like I'd dreamed?)
But there was Marilyn
putting into perspective
the path I'd taken.

Our roads converged
the summer
my father died.
I needed her perspective.

Living Life in Boxes

"So, out at the beach this weekend
instead of grading our papers, eh?"
Phyllis said, no harm intended
by her gently sarcastic quip.
Phyllis was older than me;
we often joked after class.
She thought she knew
it'd be okay
to make an
off hand remark.

I intended no harm with my answer,
only the truth:
"My father died on Saturday."
        It was raw.
        I was raw.
        He was my rock.
        I taught my class that day
        because my father would
        have wanted me to.
        Commitment.
        Dedication.
        Doing your job:
        That's what we did.

        We live our lives
        in little boxes.
        I told no one else.

Couldn't have held up
if I did. Just teach.
And go home and cry.

I guess Phyllis felt guilty and apologized.
I don't recall. She shared the next day
that she'd spent time with her aging parents.

Neither of us ever said, but I suspect
neither of us ever forgot that moment.

Deductive Logic

If I want future teachers
to love books
Then they need to read
A lot.
If I want my students to remember
One hundred books.
Then they need to write about them—
One hundred reviews.
If I ask undergrads to do that much work
Then some will plagiarize.

If a student, once confronted, meets with me
Then there are tears. Always tears.
"I've never done this before," the student sniffs.
"And obviously I'm not very good at it, since I got caught."

If a twenty-year-old writes in her review:
"When I read this book to my grandchild, she loved it."
Then you know she didn't even read
before she cut, pasted, and plagiarized.

Among my fat files of plagiarism forms,
some stories are the stuff of lore,
shared each semester to warn
each new crop of future teachers:
If you plagiarize in the computer age
Then you're going to get caught.

Stopping Cheating One Sad Evening

Whose words these are, I think I know.
Ideas, I'd say, from some odd fellow.
My students, all, must find it strange
no matter how much they rearrange—
I, from a Google search, detect
words that aren't from their intellect.
Alas, I don't give them a break—
I let them know there's a grave mistake.
This, the darkest evening of their year . . .
This, the darkest evening of their year.

Recommendation Letters

Here's the irony:
Having no idea what to write
when that very first request came:
"Would you write me a letter of recommendation?"
I did what I always do—sought a model.
Back in the Dark Ages before internet to Google it,
I found the letter my major prof had written
for my grad school application.
True confession: I plagiarized
one of the lines. It was so perfect,
so perfectly complementary.
No one would ever know.
And they didn't.
Until now.

I've written hundreds of letters
for job applications, for grad school, for scholarships.
I know it's a hard request to make.
After all, students assume
you'll be willing to say good things.

Only three times did I qualify (or refuse) the request.
For one future teacher, I said I could write the letter
but would acknowledge her non-standard English.
Thanks for your honesty but no thanks.

For another, applying to grad school in philosophy,
I said he'd be better served by a prof in his major field.
Why would he even ask? Didn't he recall
that for fifteen weeks, I labored in vain

to break his propensity to write one-hundred-word sentences
which obfuscated any point he was trying to make?

For a third, who'd been virtually silent
in my discussion class
whose teaching video showed him
rooted to his spot, stiff,
uncomfortable in his skin,
lecturing endlessly.
I declined.
Honesty is a hard call.

The Undereducated

Week after week
the marks and comments
on Layla's papers
pointed out problems:
grammar, spelling,
sentence structure,
shallow ideas (Tell me more)
mangled meaning (Unclear, please explain).

Then came the outburst:
"I'm not even sure I should be here."
(I wasn't sure either.)
How can a person teach
kids the very things
she doesn't know herself?
Which I sort of said.

You've been cheated
all your life, I told her,
of the education you deserve.
No one held you
to a high standard,
demanded what you're
capable of. You *can*
meet that standard
if you want to.
Yes, you have gaps to fill.
But you can do it
if you believe in yourself.
And if you put in the time.

Three, four, five times,
this scenario played out.
The students cried—
said they wanted to improve.

"*I* believe in you if
you believe in you,"
I'd say.

Some made it.
Some did not.

Stealing from Students

For her night as discussion leader,
Pallie slowly, deliberately, and mysteriously
unpacked a brown bag brimming with groceries—
grapes clinging to the vine,
papaya hiding its seeds within,
figs, guava, and cantaloupe,
an onion ready to unveil its layers,
almonds, plums, and peaches,
potatoes with eyes watching us,
avocado's ugly rind enclosing its huge pit,
asparagus banded together in solidarity.

"Can you guess where
I'm going with this?" Pallie asked.

"The chapter titles of the novel!" Jenn hollered.

"Indeed." Pallie smiled. "And your job
is to harvest the symbolism."

We cut, we peeled, we tasted, discovering
so many layers we had not seen
in our first draft reading of *Esperanza Rising*.

"I am so stealing this lesson plan,"
I told our indomitable leader.
That was 2003, and each year since
Pallie's legacy lived on.

Shout Out

This is for you quiet students
        who shrink in a corner,
        determined to stay hidden
        not called out or called on.

This is for you want-to-share-but-slower-to-speak
        who never get your say because
        the tide of conversation has already turned
        by the time your words are warmed up.

This is for you overthinkers whose thoughts
        bubble up like Macbeth's witches' brew
        but you stay silent to avoid trouble,
        not stirring the pot.

This is for you quick-to-share dominant speakers
        learning (because I told you): Tone it down,
        count to ten before you speak,
        open space and listen.

This is for you silence breakers for whom
        I am grateful. If you didn't shoulder
        the mantle of responsibility, I'd have to
        answer my own questions.

This is for you worriers who wonder
        if you belong in college. You know you
        have far to go and you're working
        to get there. You will.

This for you all: Know that one day, you'll be
    shouting out to your own students
    with the hope that you'll remember
    everything you were and were not
    as a student so you won't expect
    your students in your own image.

Staying Late at the Office, August 26, 2005

Just two of us were still
in our offices late
on a Friday afternoon
the first week of classes.

When Sheehan called down the hall
and mentioned Katrina
I asked, "Katrina who?"
thinking we may both
have this mutual student.

"That storm in the gulf,"
she called. Who knew then
that the storm in the gulf
would upend our lives?
That we would not return
to campus for five months.

That we would be scattered
to the winds, wondering if
we had jobs, if
we had houses, if
our students were safe, if
we'd survive
the devastation of our city.

A Job Deferred

Many moons ago,
there had been one
other volunteer job
in my rehearsal phase of
searching for life's work—
a summer gig with my mother
in the Earl K. Long Library.
Did I mention I love libraries?

Though I cherished time
spent with my mother,
the possibility perished
under humdrum tasks. I crossed
librarian off my "dreaming-
about-the-future" list
—or did I?

What happens to a dream deferred?
It explodes.

Thirty years after said volunteer gig,
when a UNO colleague in charge
of the Children's Library retired,
I took on its care and feeding,
tending and weeding,
a labor of love.
Did I mention how much I love libraries?

Thirteen Ways of Looking
at a Library Collection

I
After Hurricane Katrina's flood waters
lay waste to libraries,
heaps of sodden volumes
piles of rusted shelving
dotted the landscape, once loved books
mere mush at school's curbsides.
I volunteered for the daunting task
to help rebuild one collection,
Hynes Library in Lakeview.
Where to begin?

II
Partner with people
passionate about books.
I tapped my library science students,
lucky enough to have been privy
to the passion of one in particular
Hynes newly minted librarian, Chris,
who took not one but five of my courses.
Our roles were many.

III
As architects
we started with a blueprint.

IV

As builders
we started with a foundation.

V

As data gatherers and interpreters,
we met with teachers
thought through curriculum,
thought through events of a school year,
thought through wants and needs of the kids.

VI

We learned to "do the Dewey"
(so dubbed by Elaine, former student
and librarian par excellence)
a dance with knowledge
from 000s to 900s.

VII

As explorers, we followed
every tributary that flows
into the river of knowledge.

VIII

As culture bearers,
we were diligent in efforts
to be sure every kid
could see themselves
on the pages of the books they read.

IX

We stood on shoulders of giants
(so trite, so true) trusting reviewers
and myriad librarians and booklovers
who have served on award committees
who read and read and read
to select the absolute best.

X

As archeologists, we excavated,
dug for relics
headlamps on
late into the night.

XI

At long last
we stood before the gates
of our castle of books.

XII

And let the kids in.

XIII

Had such joys of a librarian's job
tickled my fancy so many moons ago,
my life's journey might have been different.
How fickle the fates
that land us where they do.

Book Fairy

Sometimes
you sow
seeds that need
rich soil
before
roots grow deep
before
you see
how the flowers bloomed
and spread their own seeds.

Lauren was such a seed.
Who knew she'd become the Book Fairy
gathering books like squirrels gather nuts
giving them away on special book days.
Every kid in her school, touched by her
fairy dust, builds a home library.

When I learned of her Riviere Readers project
I joined her squirrel team and donated weeded books:
"These aren't all that good," I warned.
"No worries," she assured me.
"In a book desert, all books are good books."

Lessons Learned . . . Again

Reading *A Wreath for Emmett Till*
I am always amazed
that most white students
        never heard Till's name
all Black students
        know his story well.

Shontell airs frustration
wondering aloud:
"Have my people done nothing
since the civil rights movement?
Must we revisit this pain
when we read about African Americans?"

She wants to raise her daughter, she says
to be strong
to know heroes
        who invented things
        who made discoveries
not just heroes from the civil rights era
not just slave narratives. Her heartfelt words
spawn a deep spontaneous reckoning:
        What do we select
        for teens to read
        and why?

I have heard this before. . . . (Remember Craig?)
I should have known this—
I am a slow learner.
Shontell shouldered the pain
so her white prof and white peers might hear.

(To Sid)

He hid behind
his computer
in the cavernous classroom
against the wall
near the folding partition
that almost obscured him.
Sat silent, rarely a remark—
no, never a remark.

Yet I knew
that insights lurked
emerging as they
did in parenthetic asides in journals.
He'd been drawn in, he said,
when I spoke of my childhood
"before the Punic Wars."
(English majors love allusions.)
And so we forged
a parenthetic friendship.

Multicultural Education

Each class member took the lead
discussing one of the readings.
Who, I wondered,
would pick white privilege?

Not James, former navy man
self-described as trailer park trash.
Flat out announced: *White privilege isn't a thing.*
He believed in meritocracy.

Brave soul to select the topic was Claire who,
I later found out, was the student wondering on day one:
"What can I learn about multicultural education
from all these white people?"

Now That The Testing Is Over

Sydney's smile spread a mantle of joy
over the class as she pronounced,
"Now that the testing is over I can teach what I want."

Teachers inundated with mandates
wonder why they went into teaching to begin with.
That is, until April. Then the good teachers,
who have listened all year long to kids' questions,
dig in to what their charges really want to know:
about planets, about dinosaurs…
The power of choice we preach in education classes
becomes possible and projects abound
only when testing is over.

I admit it: I teach teachers
not for the schools as they are
but for the schools as they should be.

Other People's Stories

Sydney's classroom walls were adorned
with a portrait of America's First Family.
(And Sydney loved when her first graders
told her she looked like Michelle Obama.)

It was fall 2016 and in social studies class,
they talked about elections.

"I don't think Trump likes my people,"
said a Muslim child.

"No, baby, I don't think he does," said Sydney.

"I don't think he likes your people either,"
said the same savvy six-year-old.

Legacy

My students,
future teachers, fill me
with their stories, which
I pass along to other students.

Jasmine, who taught at a Baptist preschool,
read *Mommy, Mama, and Me*
to her two- and three-year-old class
much to the consternation of her principal.
He questioned her
book choice about two mommies
questioned her
challenging the beliefs
of the church.

"Are you saying that you want me to teach hate?" she asked.

Case rested.
Enough said.
Jasmine's story was
her legacy ever after
when I taught about censorship.

Discovering Deficits

Reading aloud to kids
may come naturally to some.
But most future teachers need coaching—
    where to pause to make meaning
    how to phrase to make music
    when to stop and ask questions
    what to emphasize to engage and
    keep listeners hanging
    on every word.
When coached, magic happened,
at least most of the time.
Sentence by sentence,
page by page parsing
what matters.

But other times
coaching revealed a deep crevasse
far beyond being an expressive reader.
Sadie did not know
when the Civil War was fought.
"1920s?" she guessed.
"1940s?" she amended after
one look at my face.
"No," I countered.
"That was World War II."
"I'm not good with dates," Sadie said,
an embarrassed laugh hiding in her words.
"The CIVIL War," I said louder
as if volume would help.
Nothing.

Trying another angle, I asked who
was president during the time of slavery.
Another embarrassed laugh.
     She actually
     didn't know.
"I never was good
with history," Sadie said.
     No kidding.

Twenty years old.
Would be certified to teach
in two short years.

Nonreaders

First day of class

There was Matt
future math teacher who admitted
signing up and dropping the class
signing up and dropping the class.
No eleventh-hour escape now.

There was Grant
"I have no idea how I'll survive this class."
The ten towering novels,
a Sisyphean task.
He couldn't remember the last time
he'd read a whole book.

There was Sahid
"English isn't my first language."
He worried. "And I never read
as a kid anyway."

There was Meaghan
late to read as a child,
never read to,
never enjoyed books,
self-described math person.

"You're a dad," I told Matt.
"Read to your kids."

"You're a musician," I told Grant.
"Listen to the musicality of the words.
Listen to the novels to manage
time and lessen fears."

"You *do* like stories," I told Sahid.
"I hear your deep thoughts
about books we share.
I believe in you.
Believe in *yourself*."

By semester's end….
"Where were all these books all my life?" Matt wondered.
"Thank you," wrote Grant, "for making me a new reader."
Sahid relished his slow slog to victory.
Overachieving Meaghan read to reach one hundred but didn't stop.
First undergrad in two decades
to surpass reading two hundred books in one semester,
and she loved them.

Storytime and stories
wound tendrils around
these new readers
and changed them.

On Observing a High School English Class

"I want you to think
about things that
really matter to you,"
Jane posed to her twelfth grade poets.

Heads bowed (mostly).
Some gazed, eyes
tracking the teachers—
not quite believing
that we were writing too.

Thoughts emerged—
students feared the future
they will face,
unprepared as they are,
Josue said,
to do taxes or
understand mortgages
because school
has failed them.

They didn't worry
about x and y
but wondered why
xy axes consume
so much time
when time better spent
could help them
know their rights
to fight against

what frightens them:
Louisiana, their state, loses
two football fields
of land every hour
to wetland erosion.

Cameron asked
what socialism is
because forms of government
weren't taught,
or if they were,
so briefly, so dryly
it didn't sink in.

Cameron considered too
how his generation
looked through the window
that the first Black
president opened.

Heads bowed,
pens moving.
Silence and stillness
were their tools
as they puzzled
what matters—
capturing their concerns
in slam poetry.

YES!

Progress

"I'd never share that filth with children,"
Bryan exploded—
slamming books on the table,
storming from the room.
I had just read *Daddy's Roommate*.
It was 1999. Thirty years after the Stonewall riots.

The class sat in stunned silence
before the brave few spoke up:
"I'd share the book with kids."
Most admitted they would not.

2019, fifty years after the Stonewall riots,
more than half of my class voted *George*
a novel about a transgender child
as the winner of the Mock Newbery—
most distinguished contribution to American Literature.
Let's hear it for Gen Z.

Disrespected

"Can I talk to you after class?" Alison asked.
(*Oh, great,* I thought. *My born-again homophobe.*
What now?)

Alison had refused to read *George.*
"And what will you do," I had asked,
"if you have a trans kid in your class?"
"I'll treat all children equally,"
she swore on her stack of bibles.
She still requested a different book.
I gave her *Totally Joe.*
"It might help you understand your brother,"
I said. Don't know if she read it.
She skipped the class discussion.

"So, what's up?" I kept it casual.
Conversational. Friendly, I hope.
"You disrespected me last Thursday."
"Because...?" I asked.
"When you corrected me
when I said my brother
chose to be gay."
"But being gay *isn't* a choice," I said.
Again. "It's an identity."
"In your world, not in mine," she insisted.
Alison carried on:
"My values,
my religion . . ."
Blah blah blah.

I listened.
I nodded my head.
She was right
of course, about one thing:
I would never understand
people like her.
I will never really believe
she could respect
every student
in her future
class.

Just What I Needed to Hear

"Don't think we haven't noticed,"
Thomas told me,
"how inclusive you are
how alongside the books and discussions
about immigrants, about trans kids,
about civil rights activists,
you still lean in to listen
to the students with Trump stickers
slathered on their laptops,
to the students with Jesus
tattooed on their arms."

Searching

On the penultimate week of classes,
I'm on duty at the circulation desk
in my haven—the children's library.
I watch Helena search
the electronic catalog,
jot a list of titles,
briefly search shelves,
and sit back down—

with no books.

"How did you do—finding your books?
I ask.
"I couldn't find a single one."
A pause.
"I don't understand the system,"
she says.

Found out
she'd spent an entire semester
mostly googling titles
and listening
to someone online read them.
After fifteen weeks of class in a library
after fifteen weeks surrounded by books
she's not at home
in this space.

Sigh.

Back to the drawing board
planning next fall's course.
How do I get Googlers
excited
capable
comfortable
in a library?

Confidences

Steven always had a lot to say,
so much that peers
sometimes rolled their eyes
when he held forth
a font of information,
a spate of opinions.
(He was an expert on bullying.)
Slight of build, he stood
just over five feet tall.

In the quiet of the library,
he talked about his fiancé in Paris
their plans for summer.
His conversation rambled,
reached out. A pronouncement one day
"I used to be a girl."

    *   *   *

Amina's eyes were cast down
as she waited to see me alone after class.
"I'm sorry I did not write much
about this week's novel.
It was too close to home."
She paused.

"I'm sorry," I said. "That has to be hard."
Deep eyes brimming with tears,
Amina continued. "I was abused too."
"I'm so sorry," I repeated,

words failing me.
She just stood there,
the silence heavy surrounding us.

"My cousin raped me, has raped me
  since I was nine years old.
  I never told anyone before."
"Oh, Amina . . ."
  She just stood there,
  the silence heavier surrounding us.

"Can I give you a hug?" I asked.
She nodded.

          *   *   *

Children's books opened spaces.
They ushered invitations
to my students
to seek someone out,
to let someone in—
into their pasts, their pain.
I was honored to be the someone.

Monika

Email is a constant for professors.

Some missives stop you in your tracks:

I wanted to email you before classes start to see if I can meet with you about how my condition could affect my approach to your class. This past year I have been under chemotherapy since I had surgery in October 2016 for a glioblastoma (malignant brain tumor). I am still under chemotherapy, but I am trying to graduate this May. Because there's still no cure for glioblastoma, the dose of chemo I receive is tripled and that keeps me in bed the first 8-10 days of each round.

Some students stop you in your tracks.

With every reason to wallow in self-pity,
Monika instead mirrored
a prism of optimism,
illuminating a spirit
deep inside of
compassion
dedication
inspiration
for me, for others, that we might at least try
to see the world through her eyes—
a kaleidoscope of hope.

The Weight of Stories

"So," I asked Amy. "What brought you to teaching?"
"I always loved kids and couldn't have them," she said.

(Why had I even asked that question?)
Actually, I knew why. It was
a casual conversation starter the first day
when she was the first student in the room.
Her answer was anything but casual.

Her truth
her trust
hit hard
(I'd wanted kids too: never had them.)

What had I said back to her?
I cannot recall.
Why did she think that I'd asked her
that question. Was she worried
that I thought she was older? (I wasn't.) What if
she worried that I thought she didn't fit in?
(I didn't.)
In her confidence to me,
did she feel I sensed
her lack of confidence?

That truth
that thought
that knowledge
of her life of loss
was only the first

that would emerge.
Her bare truth
wrapped in a veil of sadness
sensed, not said
would unfold all semester
in things she wrote
in connections she made
in response to the books she read.

The sadness surrounded
her whole life.
Depression
Treatment
(Some of which harmed
more than helped.)

The first week, she shared that one story.
The last week, through poems
she shared so many more stories—
lost her brother when she was nine
lost her father when she was thirteen
fearful now she would
lose this chance to change life's path and teach
because she couldn't pass
the damned math test,
which was prerequisite to the program.

Her stories hung heavy on my heart.

Graduation

Over twenty-five years
watching 25,000 thousand-plus graduates,
one graduation melds into another.
One stands out.

As we headed to the stage
where I would bestow
Desi's doctoral hood, she whispered
"Let's do it all over again."

For Dr. Desi (with a nod to George Ella Lyon)

You are from an appointment, observing one of my classes.
Exchanging thoughts about your goals, we sensed an
   immediate bond.
You are from the summer of bread and books
from Aristotle, Dante, and their secrets,
an illuminated summertime.

You are from Paulo Freire, Nel Noddings, bell hooks
from your song cycle capturing women's ways of knowing
that shed understanding and evoked tears—
you were on your way to discovering you.
You are from the Dust Bowl,
and a mother's pain,
from literature, listening, and loving learning.
You are from igniting basic writers
and sparking seasoned ones.
You are from endless planning, from brewing coffee,
brewing conversations, and bookmaking.
You are from Sydney and high stakes tests
and teaching about dinosaurs.
You are from being a musician before you were a teacher,
a teacher before you were a researcher.
You are from poetry, piano, visions, and voice.

You are from an invitation
to do whatever your heart desired
from moments and memories,

from a litany of lyrics,
and making magic happen
again and again.

For Nikki (who ordered this poem)

I read to my Children's Lit students
about Judy, Nelson, and Sherry
from this loosely linked collection
of verse that you are now reading.
Then read about Tasha
and her father's murder.

An unsettled quiet
settled over the class.
"Who wrote that?" Nikki asked.
"I did," I said—
which in a way was a lie.
I had only recognized
that Tasha's words
those many years ago
were a poem
and wrote them down.
More silence.

But Nikki broke that silence:
"I want you to write poems about us."

A Father's Critique Revisited

"Why are you always changing jobs?"
my father had often asked me.
Fast-forward many years
beyond my father's death.
I want to tell him: See, I found
the perfect fit with college kids:
Twenty-six years in one place.
Daddy would be proud.

Epic Failure

Failure sucks
the psychic energy
from a semester.
Yes. Even after forty-six years.

Sure, risks were taken:
Start-up school, uncertified faculty.
But plans were laid
and hopes were high.

Six future teachers
would engage ninth graders
in book club discussions
of Angela Johnson's *The First Part Last.*
Such potential to offer teens
mirrors and windows.

Wrong.

There was little engagement
and fault lay on all sides:
overwhelmed faculty abdicating involvement,
awkward college kids with no teaching presence,
too many high school kids with PTSD,
and me
haunted by memories
of Barbre Junior High.

Tanka for New Semesters

Beginning again
I am out of step until
I find life's rhythms
The burdens in students' lives
keep me awake, worrying

Haiku for Accreditation

Decipher jargon
meetings of planning to plan
sacrifice our souls

Square pegs meet round holes
endless data collection
signifying naught

Gen Z Anxiety

Bobbi took me up on my offer
to drive those without transportation
to a school to read to children.
From a rural parish,
she was afraid,
      it turns out,
of driving in the city.

She was afraid of much more,
      I discovered
when we chatted about Gen Z.
"The great thing
about your generation," I said,
"is tolerance, acceptance
of differences.
But on the other hand,
so many Gen Z students
are on drugs for anxiety."
"I am," she said.

"Is social media to blame?" I asked.
"Absolutely," she said.
"Where is the anxiety coming from?"
I wondered aloud.
"There's so much evil in the world,"
she confided.
I hadn't thought this through.

When they were born—
in the year of Columbine

When they grew up—
with Newtown,
Aurora, Parkland, Pulse,
Emanuel AME Church.

Schools and churches:
                    Not safe.
Going to the movies:
                    Not safe.
Going to a club:
                    Not safe
Made sense:
So much evil in the world.

Almost Affirmation

In our weekly class ritual
we begin with storytime.
Each grad student
takes a turn, and in turn,
we critique: "She kept my interest."
"She used great voices for different characters."

Our words should be different,
I knew,
the night Lydia read.

After they read, I modeled:
"Their decision to have us
on the rug was perfect and involving,
and they chose a great book."
A student piped up: "Her voice
in the repeated refrain was soothing."

"I would happily be a four-year-old
in her classroom," I added.

DAMN.
I *almost* got it right
But not quite.

I scrawled in written critique:
Great job with your read aloud.
I'm so sorry for messing up on pronouns.

Lydia later emailed—

"Thanks for your comments," they wrote.

"It means so much. I am still navigating pronouns."

PART V

BRAVE NEW ONLINE WORLD
A HERO'S JOURNEY

Call to Adventure 2005

In the time of Katrina,
  the call to online adventure came
    scattered
        by wind and water,
as we were,
    across the country.

In the time of Katrina,
  I was the one
    colleagues and friends
        doubted would even leave
    the threatened city.
  I was the one
    who had made a choice
      to leave
    my laptop behind.

Didn't want to privilege technology
  as if it were more
      important
        than everything else
        I had to leave
Just in case the worst happened.

October 2005   we were asked
to remotely   resume our classes.

Refusal of the Call

In the time of Katrina
     sans internet
     sans computer
     sans phone
I had no choice
     really was glad
to have no choice.

I refused the call.

My students whom I'd met for one day
     whose papers evacuated with me stashed
     in my satchel stayed untouched.
My students became someone else's students.

A Second Call 2020

In order for the University to test its course continuity readiness, we will hold a one-day drill on Thursday, March 12. All scheduled in-person classes on that date will be conducted remotely. All faculty members are expected to communicate with their students and follow through with course instruction.

In the time of Corona,
          when the call to adventure came
          on a Tuesday
I had no choice.

                    I answered the call.

I left the ordinary world
I'd inhabited for more than four decades
and entered a special world
          where the ground shifted beneath my feet,
          where my nemesis Technology
beckoned. With fear and trembling
          I rose to meet it.

          I   the luddite
          the butt of jokes at faculty meetings—
          "Let's put Pat in charge." They laughed
          as they posited creating a department
          Facebook page. (Guess they guessed
          my stance and absence on social media.)

          I   the luddite who scoffed
          at colleagues who said, "We

have to offer online classes,
online degrees to be competitive
in the higher ed market."

I   the luddite who declared
          I'll retire
before I teach online . . .
headed online
for the one-hour crash course
on facing my foe.

"What are the differences
between forum, open forum, and chat?"
I asked. "What's Panopto?"
          How do I set up this and that?
Dared I hope I could Zoom?
          (which, at least, was on my radar)
  "Asynchronous is better," they warned.
"We can't all Zoom at once."

"Good questions, Pat," a colleague wrote in the chat,
"You know you're going to blow your luddite cover."

"Yeah, right," I replied.

Let's say, I was
          a bit panicky
Let's say, I was entering
          not just a special world
          but freak out mode

until I met my mentor.

Meeting My Mentor

No, it was no one new
but someone I knew—
my guide through life: my sister.
Already socially distanced from
        the twenty-first century
no computer
no devices
no tech savvy
She was not my technical guru
        but instead restored
        my belief in me.

Even when my endless chatter
about all-things tech was a sea
        of nonsense,
        she listened.
"You've been through Katrina,"
she said. "You'll get through this.
Think of it as an adventure."

Crossing the Threshold

After internal brainstorming
after reviewing the syllabus
after wondering how course content translates
      out of our comfort zone
      out of our daily routines
after twenty-four hours
      I launched an online forum.

Invitation to undergraduate
Children's Literature students:
Rocket into cyberspace.
  Chart the stars of the children's book world
      via authors' and illustrators' videos—
         share your thoughts.
            Let me know if you have questions.
I mapped the path
    showed the way
      hoped they would follow.

Tests

The first sign of life
in this brave new world
came Thursday before noon
from Hannah:

Dr. Austin,
I don't have any questions or anything but I just wanted to
thank you for being my first and only teacher so far to email a
game plan for this craziness going on. You seem so flexible and
prepared even though I'm sure this is super stressful on all the
faculty. Thank you for putting us first! (Not that other teachers
aren't. You're just the best at it.) We will figure this mess out as
a class!

I passed my first test.

Test number two: the graduate class.
Invitation to inquiry online.
Would it even be possible
to create asynchronously
            (Who even knew this term?)
a conversation we might have
face to face?
            (Who even fathoms threads
            of conversation that spin out
            over a whole week?)
Would I proffer questions
that spark discovery?

What is the value of folklore? I posed.
How are its characters different
than the characters that people
picture books, novels,
and our ordinary world?

They came through
as students do.

And the world of fairy tales was,
            it turns out,
            the perfect place
to venture into the current
            dystopian universe
where we all face
horrible things in our lives.

As characters in fairy tales
face monsters, we face
difficult people, difficult situations.
We're facing one now, I wrote,
with Corona.
We want to know
we can come out
on the other side,
vanquishing that monster.
That's a huge part
of the value of folklore.

In asynchronous response Lydia wrote:

I love thinking about dealing with difficult situations and people in this light. I think that is why this particular coronavirus situation has been so unnerving. We're looking for what exactly will vanquish this monster, and unfortunately, the only thing to vanquish it may be to sit home and wait. I think the message of good reigning over evil is so important even if we don't know what will happen next in our lives. Even if we don't see a lot of good reigning. Maybe just believing in that possibility is part of what helps us through!

To give credit where it was due
I footnoted my source
nine asynchronous days later.

The analogy of monsters-in-our-lives
to fairy tale monsters came
via Eric Kimmel, reteller of tales,
who came by this insight via a friend
who ferried Eric through a dark time
who then shared it in a symposium.

Because of my allies (my students),
because of Kimmel's words
returning to me at the right moment

I passed another test.

Twin Terrors

I

More tests, bigger tests—
twin terrors descended the very next day.
University email: *Beginning on Monday, March 16, and
until further notice, all in-person classes will be delivered
remotely.*

Why had I hoped the "test drill" would be just one day?
   Why had I dared think we would return to normal?
      Why did I not see this coming? That the future
      was now.

The promise of   six   more   weeks
Was I capable?
Could I do it?

II

Friday, March 14, 2020. I lost
connectivity.
        It was my fault.
Having received a new modem
to solve a months-old problem,
a static-filled phone line,
I faced a maze of wires
                detaching
from one
                reattaching
to the new—
                red to
red, green to
                green, yellow
to yellow.

At first it appeared
                to work.
Until it didn't.
        Internet silent
                heart raced
head resounded.
        This was not happening.
        This was not happening
This   was   not   happening.

Would a call to AT&T
solve my ineptitude?
(I had only a landline.)
Lifting the receiver

I met silence.

The phone was dead.

After more panic
after hysterical tears
my mentor's land line
linked me to AT&T and yes—
they would arrive on Monday.
This
no doubt

was part of the adventure.

The Approach

A strange calm   befell

A whole weekend   without connectivity
No way to be   consumed by email
No way to see   if undergraduates
                        undertook our forum's work
No way for allies   to call and check on me

          I was
          shut off.

          Isolated.

          It was
          strangely freeing
          I gardened
          played piano
          read a book
          I didn't need to read

True calm   before Monday's storm.

The Ordeal

One asynchronous week later
and I knew—
this was not for me.

Distance learning
through forum posts felt
                              Empty
            Hollow
Distant

I liked immediacy
I wanted to see
            faces, hear voices.
I needed other choices.

How hard could it be
to host a meeting on Zoom?
            Set it up.
            Test drove.
(Thank goodness for
tech-savvy friends.
            Audio/video? Check.
            Sending invites? Check.
            Sharing screen? Check.

I was ready.

Then at five
There they were—
nine students

Smiling faces, traces
of mouths moving
But where was the sound?

(Wish I believed in prayer)

It all was proving
        I couldn't do this.

            This was not happening.
            This was not happening.

So much for trial prevention
I needed outside intervention.

Got tech-friend on the phone
thrown as I was out of my zone.

Sent out an invite so
she joined the meeting.
Couldn't hear their greetings
But watched—numb—
beating myself up inside
feeling like a jerk
hoping she'd make this work.

At first even she
had no luck. I was struck
dumb watching her try
feeling more helpless than ever
about surviving this online endeavor.
Who said I can't pray?

When all else failed,
tech-friend—
      calm problem solver
      able rescuer
set up a new meeting.

We all joined.
I stumbled through
a too quick class
aborted by time limits.

Though I was thankful for allies,
gratitude didn't minimize
my feelings of abject failure.

Rebirth

Rebirth comes with hope
and hope came from Dahlia,
(thanks, of course, to email).

*I have gotten a little emotional thinking about how much you
have already taught us in such a short period of time. I missed
everyone already on Thursday night and the mutual respect and
knowledge we share with one another in person. However, I
did enjoy our test run of the online class. I could sense everyone's
personalities through their discussions which helped me visualize
us sitting in class chatting as if it was a regular Thursday night.*

Rebirth comes with having courage
to try again
       (and again).
Within a week, Zooming
was the new normal.
Always, allies
for a teacher
are her students.

Getting a Grip: Zooming with Tommy

'Twas the morning of class
and all through the room
I was busting my ass
to go online and Zoom:

Get PowerPoint nestled all snug on the screen.
Gather picture books ready to share.
Organize notes when at last we'd convene.
Move the monitor west to avoid the glare.

Then all of a sudden, Tommy the cat
decided on a whim
he'd had too much of that.
I'd better, instead, pay attention to him.

He zoomed to the closet.
He zoomed to the bed.
"Come on," I yelled, "pause it.
There's a class to be led."

He zoomed to the cat tree
then zoomed to the floor,
zoomed all around me,
then zoomed to the door.

"Now's not the time
for your little antics."
You can imagine by now
I'm a little bit frantic.

He let out a loud meow
just to have the last word.
I finally got it.
He just wanted to be heard.

"Come on, Tommy," I said.
"Your new friends await."
Midst my pandemic dread
I cannot be late.

Wonder of wonders, he curled in my lap
as one by one, students clicked into Zoom.
Finally, I breathed: Tommy was ready to nap
to enjoy newfound fame in the quiet of his room.

More Tests, Enemies, and Allies

I
We in Luck

We in luck. We
not stuck. We

have libraries. We
beat adversaries. We

will manage. We
don't panic. They

close libraries. We
meet scary. We

assume we
are doomed.

II
Audio Haiku

Online book portal
Listening, the new reading, un-
folding treasure trove

III
Hi-tech Haiku

When my tech skills fail
and fail and fail, frustration
crescendos: implodes

IV
Uploading to My Sister

After a last-minute reread of our
        four-hanky Holocaust book
After prepping for hours and hours
        creating the perfect PowerPoint
After priming to engage my students
        get *them* talking from their silos, not *me*
After only eight of twenty students showed up
        to our Zoom meeting
After sharing my screen only to discover
        the not-edited, not updated PowerPoint version
After worrying how students experience
        class that seemed okay to me

After trying and failing to retrieve the meeting
     I thought I had recorded
After reading emails from
     a student in Georgia with tech difficulties
     a student whose husband lost his job
        wondering "How will I pay the bills?"
     a student confounded by the state's
        new regulations for intern teaching
     a student mourning the loss of Grandpa
I emerge from my home office
     ready to implode
        Again
I cross my backyard
     to my sister's house
        and upload
        all of the above.
Her listening is love.

V
Metaphysical Mysteries

Coming from the computer, sound
seems a noumenon—a thing-in-itself.

To set the mood
for my Zoom room discussion
of *Bud, Not Buddy* set in the Depression
I picked the perfect soundtrack—
the thirties "Dusky Devastators"
band music emanating into airwaves.

But, students told me, when I asked,
the sound wasn't there.
Now why?   Although I hear
        phones ring
        dogs bark
        babies babble
from *my students'* siloed spaces, they
cannot hear what I hear
        this thing-in-itself
        or so I thought,
in *my own* siloed space.

What a phenomenon—
a metaphysical mystery
What is real after all?
Kant pondered this and so do I.

VI
Quarantine Math

When you're a teacher of teachers
it's not just your own
        Inconveniences
        Aggravations
        Frustrations
        Worries
        Losses
        Grief
It's every life you touch
and every life your students touch—
inconveniencesaggravationsfrustrationsworrieslossesgrief
to the tenth power.

VII
Overwhelmed

Six weeks into quarantine i need to think
about the people who people the news i need
to think about migrants on the border
pressed together in small spaces i need
to think about the stay-at-home family
dealing with the confused kid
with Down syndrome i need
to think about the woman with parents
in stage-four Alzheimers i need
to think about those losing loved ones
unable to hold their hands i need
to be grateful to know how small
my problems are i need a mantra:
I need to be grateful
I need to be grateful
I need to be

The Road Back

I
A Dream
Dreams come in a flash
often leave just as fast.
Details crystal clear
in sleep, disappear
on waking. Not this one:
(Stay with me for the dream sequence. . . .)

Through the bustle
of familiar players
I hustle down
the familiar hall
in the Education Building,
tap on the door
of the accreditation guru.

No answer.
Turn the knob
pause a moment
open and peer in.
The desk is bare
no familiar piles
of papers strewn,
the chair   pushed back
does not sport
his familiar jacket.
     The shelves behind
do not hold
the familiar photo

of his kids.
      Had I missed the email?
      Had the guy quit?

The scene goes black
as I head back
down familiar steps
still hearing
other familiar players
knowing colleagues'
faces, voices yet
not hearing their words
and they don't seem
to see me.
Have I arrived
in this place—
these admin offices—
at closing time?
Lights out?
Locking up?
(End dream sequence)

Dreams come in a flash.
You awake just as fast
and if you remember
for more than a moment
you're left to wonder if
the dream foretold
what will be
when you return
to this place
you have not been

for six weeks
to people
you have not seen
for six weeks.

Will the accreditation
guru be gone—
the data man
who is lynchpin
in the accrediting
process we all
will face
come fall?

You're left
to wonder if
the dream is a symbol.
The blackout?
What did it mean?
Was it the end of a scene?
The end of the play
in this pandemic fray?
And what of the voices
you couldn't really hear?
Was it all about choices?
Was the dream
                not about that data guy
                              but you?
Was it: *your* empty desk
        your absence
from this place
                you do not want to face

if data is all
that matters
in the ordinary world:
      Meetings, collecting
      meaningless data
      that does not show
what you do
who you are
why you care.

Was the dream me—
running for my life
defeated by my foe
fearing the magic was gone?
Was the dream foretelling
my own quiet exit
from twenty-six years
teaching teachers?

II
Tethered

Brave new world
tethered to technology
tired of feeling stupid

III
Surreal Reality

Coping with a global
Ordeal when your own life
Really doesn't seem that different
Often brings guilt, just listening to
News that regales suffering
Around the world, in your city, in the

Very lives of the students you touch, day
In, day out as they wrestle with a
Reality both slowly and suddenly
Utterly
Surreal

IV
This New Normal

There is pleasure in our Zooming space.
There is rapture in our lives displaced.
There is togetherness as we're graced

with sharing what was before unknown.
Whether from laptop or from phone,
I see the rooms where they have grown

up, see special artwork on the wall,
hear a chorus of barking in the hall.

Amidst cats mewing
check how they're doing

Meet their babies
(Mute their babies)

But see their pride.
They, too, see a human side

of me, my cat licking my face
while, in concert, we trace

meanings of books we've read.
Reading, they have said,
combats COVID dread.

Resurrection

I

A mere six weeks before,
Hannah had despaired:
"How are we going to share
the children's books we write?"

A mere six weeks before,
I too had feared that
the sharing of student-authored books
would not be the usual
last-day ritual that invariably
sealed feelings of community.
Fortunately, I was wrong.

I shared the power
to share the screen and voila:
twenty students' stories filled our hearts.
From childhood memories to Corona woes,
we felt the feelings, admired the art.
With Zoom's "chat function" shared applause,
put all our current pain on pause.

Echoing my own satisfaction,
a final seal of approval came
soon after class
when Joella wrote:

*I thought everyone did such a fantastic job that, on behalf of
my classmates, I will say thank you, Dr. Pat. It was your input.
It was your knowledge. It was your love for books. It was your*

love for us that we all did so well. You brought the best out of us as a class, as well as individuals. You tapped into something in us that some of us probably did not even know that we had. You have a gift. Take a bow, Dr. Pat. If I ever decide to write my own life story, I promise that you'll be there between the lines on the pages filled with hope and encouragement. But even if I don't, you have already written a special page in my heart.

I wept happy tears
to read these words.

Every single student
had already written
special pages on *my* heart.

Resurrection
II

My lesson plan for the final night
of my graduate class—
student-led read alouds—
was sparse at best. It would take as long
as it would take. I was fine with lite.
Almost didn't care if I didn't finish strong.

Never could I have planned
on our less travelled road,
how way would lead to way when Caitlin
asked us to think about routines
and read us *There's a Cow in the Road!*—
      a silly book about a girl
      getting ready for school
      only to be faced
      with a litany of woes
      all beginning with a cow in the road.
An awkward silence followed
Caitlin's way-too-serious question:
"How does the protagonist
navigate life's obstacles?"

I'm not sure we saw, at first, that a silly book
has a theme. But a dam burst as we considered
the necessary humdrum of routine vs.
the sacred nature of ritual
      both crucial
      as we wend
      our ways through days.

Had we all not just faced our own cows?
The most bizarre of all imaginable things?
This pandemic—ripping us from routines
tossing us into the sea of distanced learning?
       Yet we navigated indeed.
       Swam and survived.

Never could I have planned
on our less travelled road,
how way would lead to way
as Renee asked us to say
things we were passionate about:
       "Think of the a-ha moment
       that led you to that passion.
       Write your passions in large letters
       and hold them high," she said.
And on our screens
in our postage-sized portraits
we penned our passions:
mental health, art, reading scripture,
gardening, cooking, teaching,
running, reading,
reading, art.

My sign, might you guess, said teaching.

Although I did not share details
of my a-ha moment leading to teaching
I knew it was a moment in retrospect.
First, some sixty years ago
had come that vehement declaration
about my future:

But never a teacher.
Yet, some sixty years ago was the seed,
planted but not sown, that would grow
to my passion. And the seed (no surprise)
came from a book—the life of Helen Keller.
It wasn't young Helen but Anne Sullivan
who inspired the seed. How I wondered
did she break through Helen's silence?
How did she bring light to the darkness
giving the gift of language?

It was long after I'd stumbled
onto the teaching life that
this realization came—that the seed,
planted then at ten, would take root
and that the roots would strangle
the notion of never wanting my world
to be classrooms and kids.
Ironic that the book Renee read aloud
was *The Night Gardener*.

We ended the course compiling
our virtual collaborative book, each
reading our own "Where I'm From" poem,
        (Thank you, George Ella Lyon)
bonding even more over memories.

Class photo. Screenshots.
(Thank you, Dahlia,)
and we were down to the final farewell:
"I don't want to say goodbye,"
Renee said. "You hang up first."

Return with the Elixir

As I clicked, "Leave meeting. End for all."
As I lowered the lid of my laptop
the final night of the final class—
how do I even begin to describe
the rosy glow enveloping me?

How do I translate triumph, if you will,
over technology—the end, *I hoped,*
of the venture into the brave
new online world?

As I headed to bed
I tried on phrases
to describe the feeling . . .
drug-induced high?
alcoholic's buzz?
Even stepped back in time—
a Rocky Mountain High?
None quite right.

Then it dawned:

Return with the elixir—
which Noah Webster claims—
        an essential principle
which Joseph Campbell claims—
        enlightenment
        the all-healing elixir
        of inner change.

I understood
the final step
of the hero's journey
in a way I'd never
known before:
    I claimed the confidence
        to create community
            whatever the platform.

My students and I
started the semester
as strangers
coming together
from individual spaces
to sacred classroom spaces.
Despite our altered path,
        midway through,
to quarantined places, we
wove parallel plots
        of our lives
sustained the bonds
        we had found.

No teacher
takes a journey
alone.

No teacher
is a hero
of her own
story.

My heroes?
My fellow travelers
on this journey.

PART VI

RETROSPECTIVE

Turning Point

A message that will live in infamy:
July 1, 2020
Email from my boss
New directive: All classes thirty and larger MUST be online

Pat,

I am sorry that we cannot offer classes face to face as you prefer but the administration is concerned about student and faculty safety. I wanted to let you know so that you can prepare for the fall semester.

Seven weeks in spring I had survived
when we were suddenly forced online.
> Because I knew the students
> Because we were already a community

But fifteen weeks?
Meeting students online?
> No.

Could I do it?
> Yes.

Been there.
Proved that.

Did I want to do it?   No.

All those hassles?
All that screen time?   No.

Was it time?

Already since May
I'd slipped into a writing life.
My preparation for fall
       (Retirement?)

I barely admitted the possibility to myself
let alone to anyone else.

Saying it aloud made it too real.

Immediate Aftermath

The decision
to end a career
that is who you are
    is a death
    and it is lived
in stages of grief—
grief that defies linear progression
grief that morphs moment to moment
    from sadness to acceptance
    to bargaining, to denial
    to reflection, to relief
    to hope
back to sadness about
new teaching years
beginning without me.

Who would be behind me doing the work?
Words from a student's journal
paint the picture of that work:
Joella wrote of two favorite books,
The War That Saved My Life and *Each Kindness:*

*They prodded the sleeping bear in my spirit, one that I thought I
put to rest years ago. The more I read, the more the bear stirred. I
turned the pages, and he yawned. I wiped tears, and he stretched.
And when I got to a pivotal moment, all too painfully familiar
that bear awakened. He arose out of slumber with a vengeance
and ripped my soul into spiritual pieces.*

Who will be behind me knowing the books
loving the books
putting just the right book
into just the right hand
so students see themselves
so students confront discomfort zones?
I broached a former student, now Dr. Barbara
fifteen years a professor in the northwest.
Yes, the student who read
hundreds of books, thousands of books,
millions and billions and trillions of books.
"Would you be willing to teach my courses
if the university will hire you as adjunct?"

Her answer was yes.
My boss's answer was yes.

Now knowing
bibliophile Barbara
would slip into my shoes
worries slipped away.
      I owned the retirement decision.
Fellow teachers had always said:
      "You know when the time is right."
      I discovered they were right.

In Limbo

My dreams take me
into the classroom: my students—
not in the room—are on break and I
am searching for lecture notes. . . .

No mysteries here for symbolism:
File cabinet cleared out
notes in the dumpster
yet still a teacher at heart sans students.

How long will I feel
like an amputee
feeling the pain
of a remembered limb?

Haiku Quartet
Reflecting on a Teaching Life

Till soil of childhood
from clay, desert sand, rich loam
grounding their ideas

on whispers of wind
like puffs of dandelions
that land, grow, and spread

Intensify heat
sparking tinder to flame
Ignite their passions

Step into a stream
Make ripples or even waves
Sometimes change its course

EPILOGUE

Looking Back

Sifting through
snapshots of memories
I stood for a while
at the precipice of retirement
struggling
to make the leap
to end a life of deadlines
and assignments (a life
I didn't know I wanted)
I mine the past. I look back
while I still remember.

After the loss of journals and diaries
(sporadically kept over the years)
as they steeped for weeks
in Katrina's floodwaters,
locked in rusted file cabinets,
a blur of ink, I look back while
I still remember.

Without mementos and photos
(twenty-seven volumes whose images
morphed to marbleized maps of color)
drenched in the ten feet of water
that inundated my world
I look back while I
still remember.

With lurking fear that my memories
could disappear in plaques and tangles
as those of my grandmother
and mother before me
I look back while
I still
remember.

I would like to express my deepest appreciation to:

Early readers Claire Kaemmerling, Gina Billy, and Michelle Nicholson, whose comments triggered the thought that these pieces I was writing just for me might have a wider audience.

Kathleen Balma, poet and intrepid New Orleans Public librarian, who created an online pandemic writing workshop. I valued her insights as well as those of my fellow participants who weighed in on several of these pieces.

Brenda Robért, who quickly answered a critique request on rhyme and rhythm.

Members of SCBWI critique group.

Leslie Staub and Phina Schloegel, final beta readers who read and responded to the tome as a whole.

Editors Abram Himelstein, Chelsey Shannon, and G.K. Darby, for championing my work.

Alex Dimeff, designer extraordinaire, for their kindness and patience.

The thousands of students I have taught. There are so many more memorable moments than those captured here. All the students who have graced my life are here on these pages and have written a place on my heart.

On Form

Although I wrote most of the poems in free verse, I enjoyed tinkering with parody and with a few other forms including the haiku, tanka, ballad, acrostic, alphabet poem, and list poem.

Acknowledgement of inspiration:

"Childe Harold's Pilgrimage [There is pleasure in the pathless wood]" by Lord Byron – "This New Normal"

"Harlem" by Langston Hughes – "Job Deferred"

"Stopping by Woods on a Snowy Evening" by Robert Frost – "Stopping Cheating on a Sad Evening"

"Thirteen Ways of Looking at a Blackbird" by Wallace Stevens – "Thirteen Ways of Looking at a Library Collection"

"This is Just to Say" by William Carlos Williams – "Apology Poem"

"A Visit from St. Nicholas" by Clement Clarke Moore – "Getting a Grip: Zooming with Tommy"

"We Real Cool" by Gwendolyn Brooks – "We in Luck"

"Where I'm From" by George Ella Lyon – "For Dr. Desi"

The structure of the Hero's Journey from Joseph Campbell as interpreted by Christopher Vogel – Part V: Brave New Online World, a hero's journey

Quoted passage in "Mirrors":

Taylor, Mildred. *The Friendship*. Dial, 1987, 9.

Children's literature referenced:

A Wreath for Emmett Till by Marilyn Nelson, illustrated by Philippe Lardy, 2005

Are You There God? It's Me, Margaret by Judy Blume, 1970

Bud, Not Buddy by Christopher Paul Curtis, 1999

Charlotte's Web by E. B. White, 1952

Corduroy by Don Freeman, 1968

Daddy's Roommate by Michael Willhoite, 1994

Each Kindness by Jacqueline Woodson, illustrated by E. B. Lewis, 2012

Esperanza Rising by Pam Munoz Ryan, 2000

First Part Last by Angela Johnson, 2003

George by Alex Gino, 2015 (republished as *Melissa* in 2022)

Growing Up: It's a Girl Thing: Straight talk about first bras, first periods and your changing body by Mavis Jukes, 1998

Island of the Blue Dolphins by Scott O'Dell, 1960

Little Blue and Little Yellow by Leo Lionni, 1959

Mommy, Mama, and Me by Leslea Newman, 2009

Millions of Cats by Wanda Gag, 1928

Owl Moon by Jane Yolen, illustrated by John Schoenherr, 1987

Possum Magic by Mem Fox, illustrated by Julie Vivas, 1983

Snowy Day by Ezra Jack Keats, 1962

Stuart Little by E. B. White, 1945

Totally Joe by James Howe, 2005

The Family Under the Bridge by Natalie Savage Carlson, 1958

The Night Gardener by the Fan Brothers, 2016

The Secret Garden by Frances Hodgson Burnett, 1911

The Story of Helen Keller by Lorena Hickock, 1958

The True Story of the Three Little Pigs by Jon Scieszka, illustrated by Lane Smith, 1989

The War that Saved My Life by Kimberly Brubaker Bradley, 2015

There's a Cow in the Road! by Reeve Lindbergh, 1993

About the Author

Patricia Austin was born in New York City, spent her formative years in a small town in northern New Jersey, and moved to New Orleans, Louisiana, in the sixth grade. In her youth, she dabbled in lots of things. She was a dancing school and scouting dropout, lasted a bit longer with piano lessons, enjoyed people-watching, and always enjoyed creative projects. Most of all, she loved making up stories and was passionate about books and reading.

Although she never wanted to be a teacher, volunteer gigs during college years set the stage for just that possibility. As an undergraduate at Agnes Scott College, she majored in philosophy and minored in Spanish and drama. A liberal arts degree wasn't about a job but about the love of learning and discovering. Realization struck that being a jack of many trades and master of none would be a perfect fit for an elementary school teacher. She earned a Master of Arts in Teaching at the University of New Hampshire and began her career in 1973. With her eye on her dream job, teaching children's literature, she earned her Ph.D. in Curriculum and Instruction from the University of New Orleans. For forty-six years, teaching was her life's work: It fed her creative spirit. Whether with primary grade children, middle schoolers, undergraduates, master's or doctoral candidates, she nurtured her students as readers and writers.

A recipient of the Arbuthnot Award for teaching from the International Literacy Association in 2015 and the

Light Up for Literacy Award from the Louisiana Endowment for the Humanities in 2020, she has published more than fifty journal articles, several book chapters, and hundreds of book reviews. She served as reviewer for *Booklist*, co-editor of *The Journal of Children's Literature*, children's literature columnist for *Teaching and Learning Literature* as well as the Louisiana reading journal *Reading: Exploration and Discovery*. She has also served as a member of book award committees, including the NCTE committee for Notable Books for the Language Arts and the Américas Award, honoring the best in Latinx literature. Although now professor emerita, she still volunteers as curator of the Children's and Young Adult Library at UNO.

She is the author of a picture book, *The Cat Who Loved Mozart*, illustrated by Henri Sorenson, which won the Muse Award of the Cat Writers' Association, contributor to *Quilt of States: Piecing Together America* by Adrienne Yorinks and fifty librarians across the United States, and author of a collection of poetry for children, *Elephant of Sadness, Butterfly of Joy*, illustrated by Megan Elizabeth Baratta.

In retirement, she still loves dabbling in lots of things. She reads more than ever, devotes time to writing, enjoys practicing piano, has tinkered with art, and loves walking, gardening, and playing nightly games of Scrabble with her sister (her backyard neighbor). Pat lives in New Orleans with her cats, who rule her life.